SPEAKERS ON THE SPOT:
A Treasury of Anecdotes
for Coping with Sticky Situations

SPEAKERS ON THE SPOT:
A Treasury of Anecdotes
for Coping
with Sticky Situations

Edgar Bernhard

Parker Publishing Company, Inc.
West Nyack, N.Y.

© 1977, *by*

PARKER PUBLISHING COMPANY, INC.

West Nyack, N.Y.

Library of Congress Cataloging in Publication Data

Bernhard, Edgar
  Speakers on the spot.

  1. Public speaking. 2. Wit and humor.
3. Anecdotes. 4. Introduction of speakers.
I. Title.
PN4193.I5B4   808.5'1   77-22840
ISBN 0-13-824508-8

Printed in the United States of America

WHAT THIS TREASURY WILL DO FOR YOU

As public speakers, all of us have occasionally been confronted with what I call "sticky situations." Your experience with these situations to date may have been only as a spectator, but you can almost bet that sooner or later you will find yourself more personally involved. I'm referring to the times when you are introduced by the wrong name, when you are called at the last moment to substitute for the scheduled speaker, or when you are scheduled to speak to a hungry audience right *before* dinner.

During my many years as a public speaker and as a member of the audience, I've observed and experienced countless instances where a speaker was "on the spot" even before he or she had begun to speak. We all know how concerned we get about how our speech will go over. The last thing we need to worry about is something going wrong.

This treasury relieves that worry. Based on my experience, I have isolated the 60 most common sticky situations that speakers are apt to face and now present them in an easy-to-find, alphabetical sequence. Apropos of these situations are more than 250 tested anecdotes that will help you turn a potentially embarrassing moment into a crowd-pleasing opening to your talk.

Frequently you may wish to elicit questions from the audience after you conclude your remarks, so I have included appropriate ice-breaking anecdotes to encourage audience participation. Occasionally you may be faced with an embarrassing question during one of these sessions. This book enables you to handle such a situation with confidence and tact.

Another difficult situation for most speakers is when funds must be raised for one worthy cause or another. This treasury offers a choice of proven anecdotes for you to use when trying to make your audience generously receptive.

Included in this treasury is an appendix containing a selection of humorous anecdotes that you can use to enliven any speech. Over the years I've had the good fortune to hear and know many master story tellers and collectors. Drawing on these past experiences, I have chosen those stories that represent some of the best anecdotes I've encountered.

As long and as often as you have occasion to speak in public, regardless of the situation that arises, this treasury assures that you will be prepared to convert adversity into triumph.

E. B.

TABLE OF CONTENTS

TABLE OF CONTENTS

ABSENTMINDEDNESS

(You obviously forget a key detail of the meeting you are to address.)

It often happens that a speaker forgets the particular make-up of his audience, or makes an off-the-cuff remark which he immediately realizes is inappropriate, or discovers that what he said a moment ago is, for this particular audience, indiscreet. In any such situation, a flat apology is embarrassing and often makes the matter even worse. If he can make his audience smile over it, he has at least partially mended the situation—without incurring the embarrassment of an outright retraction. For example:

I must interrupt myself. Absentmindedness is an awful malady and apparently I was just afflicted by it. Sometimes one feels that he would rather be absent himself than to have his mind absent. I am almost as bad as the professor who, while walking across campus one noon, stopped a couple of students and said, "Am I walking east or west?" The students assured him that he was walking east, whereupon the professor's face lighted up and he said, "Oh, then I've had my lunch."

ARM-WAVING AND PHYSICAL GESTURES

(A previous speaker has put on a physical demonstration.)

Sometimes your speaking predecessor waves his arms, pounds the table, punches the air, and otherwise demonstrates physically, in an attempt to force his points upon the audience. In answering him, it is most important, however forcefully you may speak, that you do not imitate his wild gesturing. Instead, you might tell your audience:

Some years ago, I heard about the advice given by an elderly lawyer with years of experience to a young man who had just been admitted to the Bar. He said, "When you are arguing a case, and you know the law is against you, put all your emphasis on the facts. And if the facts are against you, remember to put all your emphasis on the law." "But," said the young lawyer, "suppose both the facts and the law are against you?" "In that case," said the older man, "you pound the table!"

When I saw my friend pounding the rostrum just now, I decided that he realized both the law and the facts are against him.

◆━◆━◆━◆━◆

Or, you may prefer to tell the audience:

Some time ago, I was sitting in a courtroom when the lawyers were making their final arguments to the jury. The plaintiff's attorney was shouting, waving his arms, pounding his fists and perspiring—so much that he interrupted himself to take off his coat and loosen his tie. When he had finished, his opponent took off his coat, loosened his tie, and *without uttering a word* began to wave his arms, punch the air, and jump up and down. After about a minute of that, he said to the jury, "I think by now I have answered all my opponent's arguments—and I would now like to present the case as I see it."

I was tempted to give you that kind of performance, but perhaps I should instead just go into my own argument without the gymnastics.

The gentleman has put on quite a show. I felt a certain lack, however, and I can best describe that lack by reminding you of a little story.

A man was lost in a wild and uninhabited region. To make matters worse, there was a terrific thunderstorm going on. He was frightened enough as it was, and the terrific peals of thunder scared him even more, but at the same time, the flashes of lightning helped him to keep on a fairly safe path. As he struggled on he began to pray, and what he said was, "Oh Lord, if it's all the same to you, could we have a little more light—and a little less noise!"

I felt that way as my friend was speaking. I am going to try to put some light on our subject and, at the same time, furnish as little noise as possible.

AUTHOR

(You are to introduce a professional writer.)

You are about to hear from a person whose latest book is now available at your bookstore. Should you buy it? You should.

I remember hearing the question, "Where has the dime novel gone?" And the answer was, "It has gone to $8.95."

I don't actually know what price the publisher has put on the speaker's latest product—but I am positive it is worth it.

◆—◆—◆—◆

In introducing our speaker, I want to remind you of something of which I know you are all aware. Writers always refer to themselves in the plural. They never say "I"; they always say "we."

The small son of a newspaper editor said to his father one day, "I know why you always say "we"—it is so that a fellow who gets insulted by what's printed will think there are too many for him to lick."

I am sure that this explanation does not apply to our speaker. He has very positive views and he does not hesitate to state them. And he will not be hiding behind any plural pronouns.

AUTHORITY

(You are to introduce a recognized authority in his field.)

When you are introducing someone who is a recognized authority in his field, you will, of course, mention that fact, as well as give supporting information such as the titles of his books, the professional periodicals in which his articles have appeared, the awards he has won, and such other forms of professional recognition as he may have had. The following story is appropriate:

Our speaker's professional eminence reminds me of the two engineering experts who fell into a highly technical dispute. After they had argued back and forth rather heatedly for some time, one of them finally said, "Let's check the *Encyclopedia Britannica* and see if we cannot resolve our differences that way." The other one readily agreed. They promptly put their hands on the appropriate volume, and the man who had suggested that they check the encyclopedia finally said, "You were right." Said the other man, "Well—that's what I *thought* I wrote."
I am sure our guest, under similar circumstances, would not be either so self-righteous or so condescending—but otherwise I can imagine his being involved in just such an incident and, if so, being able to prove his point in the same way.

◆—◆—◆—◆—◆

Mr. X is an expert in his field. Real experts are hard to come by; you don't meet one every day. Of course, you do often meet people who *believe* they are experts. For instance, consider the case of the young woman who was teaching a college class in remedial English. She gave them a rule of grammar one day, and a big fellow at the rear of the room differed with her, insisting that the rule was just the opposite. Said the teacher, "Young man, I have taught this course for three years so I think I know more about it than you." "Not at all," was the answer. "This is the third time I've had to take this course, so you see, I'm an expert in it too."

So, as I say, there are plenty of pseudo-experts. But our speaker is not one of those. You may be sure he has never had to take any course in _____ over again.

Our guest tonight is a recognized authority in his field. He has spent almost the equivalent of a lifetime in his specialty. In fact, he reminds me of a long-experienced expert in a completely different field. For many years there was a man whose sole profession was to be shot out of a cannon at every performance of Ringling Brothers Circus. One day, a newspaper reporter sought him out and asked him, "How long have you been a human cannonball?" And his smiling answer was, "Ever since I was a bee-bee."

Our speaker tonight is an acknowledged expert in his field.

Perhaps he has heard about the woman, barely able to speak English, who came into a New York bookstore and said to the clerk, "Please, I have read Senor Gunther's *Inside Europe* and Senor Gunther's *Inside Asia* and now I want to know are any more of Senor Gunther's Insides out?"

My definition of an expert is one who knows his subject inside out. I am satisfied that in a few minutes you will agree that our speaker does indeed qualify as an expert.

◆◆◆◆◆

If you are to introduce an authority in a technical field, you might include one of the following in your introduction:

> Mr. Blank is an expert. I don't know about you, but as for me, I am troubled by the fact that I may not understand him. I am reminded of the conversation between two six-year-olds. One said to the other, "What's new at your house?" And the answer was, "I just don't know. They spell everything."
>
> It's just the opposite with me. I can only hope that if he uses any technical terms, he'll remember my ignorance and he'll spell them.

◆◆◆◆◆

> Our speaker this evening is an acknowledged expert in the field of . In fact, if he uses the technical language of his specialty, it would probably be difficult for the layman to understand him. In this respect he reminds me—though he has no speech impediment whatever—of a gentleman who stuttered rather badly and went to a specialist with his problem. After about ten weeks—and difficult weeks they were—he was actually able to say clearly and without any trace of a stammer: "Peter Piper picked a peck of pickled peppers."
>
> His friends were very pleased with his accomplishment and they congratulated him on his having worked so hard and so successfully. But his answer was: "Th-th-thank you, but I f-f-find it such a d-d-difficult re-re-remark to work into the average c-c-conversation!"
>
> Our guest tonight is at home in highly technical language—language which I am sure he finds it extremely difficult to work into an ordinary conversation. That is one

reason we have made our platform available to him. The other reason is that we are very eager to hear him because we know that what he is going to tell us will be both enlightening and interesting.

BANKER

(You are to introduce a banker.)

When the speaker is a banker, it is usually true that for business as well as personal reasons he welcomes emphasis on his occupation. In introducing him, therefore, you should mention in some detail his connections with the bank and the positions he has occupied there. You may then add:

His association with the bank reminds me of the man who was looking for the Second National Bank and, unable to locate it, stopped a small boy and asked him if he knew where it was. The boy answered that he knew where the bank was and that he would take him there for a dollar. The man was in a hurry and so he quickly pulled out a dollar, gave it to the boy and said, "Take me there." The boy walked about two doors from where they were standing and said, "Here's the Second National Bank." The man said, "Isn't that a high fee for taking me such a short distance?" "Yes," said the boy, "but bank directors are paid a lot of money."

BEFORE THE ENTERTAINMENT

(You are to speak just before the meeting's entertainment.)

From the audience's point of view, if the entertainment of the evening is to follow your speech, some in the audience may look upon your talk as something that will merely delay what they came to hear. It would be well, under these circumstances, to give the audience some assurance that you are aware that the entertainment is to follow and you will not be taking too long. It would be appropriate to say:

> I want you to know that I realize I am not the entertainment of the evening, and that I am looking forward to it as much as you are. Under these circumstances, I am not willing to listen to myself for a long time—and so you won't have to either. I shall keep in mind a little rhyme I came across some time ago. Let me read it to you:
>
> What animal is most talkative?
> Has anyone kept score?
> Some people think it is the yak,
> But I think it's the boar.
>
> And since I don't want to be either one, I'll get right to the point.

BREAKING THE ICE

(You are greeting an unsympathetic audience.)

It often happens that you know in advance that the audience you will be addressing is, for the most part, not in sympathy with your views. Under those circumstances, it is best to start with an icebreaker such as the following:

> I have an idea that some of you are not in sympathy with some of the opinions I am about to share with you. I don't expect, therefore, that at the end of my talk you will all jump up on your chairs and cheer. I do expect, however, that you will fulfill the obligation of a thinking person and

not close your mind to what I am saying just because we may differ. I hope, in fact, that you will weigh my views with yours just as I would reconsider my position if our roles were reversed.

I can't help but recall at this time that on an occasion something like this, a speaker was asked in advance by the chairman how long his speech would take. He answered, "I will take about an hour, counting the time taken up by applause—but the speech itself takes about half an hour." And the chairman answered, "Well, then we'll figure on about thirty minutes over all."

I have hopes that I'm not quite in that position. But, in any case, I appreciate your hospitality and your willingness to listen.

I trust you will not decide that you are in favor of my position or against it until you have heard it! Sometimes, as you know, people decide in advance—just on the basis of what they *think* a person stands for—whether they are with him or against him. I expect that you people in this audience will not make up your minds either way until you hear what I have to say. For that, of course, I need your full attention, and how I wish I could be as successful in obtaining that as an athlete I heard about. He was a big, husky fellow, and he excelled in just one event; he was a hammer-thrower. Practically everybody knew of his prowess in that department. It was also well known that he was cross-eyed. Once, at an athletic meet, a reporter asked the coach whether he thought this man would ever become very popular. The coach answered, "Well, that's hard to say, but I'll tell you one thing—when that fellow starts swinging that hammer around, he has the attention of everyone on the field and in the stands—more than any other athlete I have ever known."

If only I could be sure of the same full attention when I am performing!

BUSINESSMAN

(You are to introduce a successful businessman.)

In introducing a leading businessman, you will, of course, give the audience pertinent facts about his education and background, and you might then wish to add the following:

In introducing Mr. _____, I am reminded of the psychiatrist who was once addressing an audience about the qualifications that fitted people for various occupations. He told of the characteristics and abilities that made for a good doctor, a good lawyer and a good businessman. And at one point he said, "The native abilities of a very good poker player are those of a very good businessman. If you ever run across a very successful poker player, you will be safe in advising him to go into business." Whereupon a man in the front row was heard to remark, "Why would a very successful poker player ever want to go into business?"

If that speaker was correct, what he said must also apply in reverse. And from what I have learned of Mr. _____'s highly successful business career, I have no desire to meet him in a poker game.

In introducing a person well known in business circles, you might wish to attribute his success in part to his sales ability, his mental dexterity and his ability to think quickly—and in that respect he reminds you of the following:

The telephone rang in a real estate office and the top salesman answered. Out of the receiver came a soft female voice asking, "Do you sell maternity clothes?" Most people would have said, "You have the wrong number," but not this top salesman. He said, "No, we don't—but you are probably going to need a larger house and I am ready to show you some bargains."

CHILDREN

(The audience includes many children.)

I am sure that some of you children have won contests. I doubt, however, that any of you have won three contests in succession, like the little girl I want to tell you about.

The first contest was for the prettiest girl in the class. She won that.

The second contest was for the most popular girl in the class. She won that.

She told her mother and father about winning those contests, and they were very proud to hear about her victories. But she never told them that she also won, the following day, a third contest. That one was for the girl who was the most stuck-up.

So you have to be careful. If you win a contest, don't let it go to your head, or you might win one you'll wish you hadn't.

CLERGYMAN

(You are introducing a minister or priest.)

A master of ceremonies or a toastmaster often finds it difficult to introduce a man of the cloth. He is likely to think that a priest ought always to be introduced very seriously; that the speaker might be very touchy and should therefore be handled with kid gloves. Almost invariably, however, a priest is more than ready to be treated in all repects like a layman, and enjoys a joke that involves his calling as much as anyone else. You might wish, therefore, to include the following in your introduction:

In presenting our next speaker, I am reminded of the young lady who was on her first trip to Europe aboard a transatlantic liner. She was excited about her trip and delighted with everything aboard ship—except for one thing: when she went to the dining room for her first evening meal on the ship, she discovered to her disappointment that she had been assigned to a table with three other women. She promptly applied to the captain, saying that she had hoped to be seated with men rather than with women, and she wondered if it would be possible to assign her to a table with three bachelors. The captain was an accommodating fellow and he said that he would certainly see to it.

And the following evening, she was guided to another table where she found that the captain had indeed complied with her request. Her new dinner companions were three very good-looking priests.

In introducing our next speaker, Dr. Blank, I want to tell him about a church revival meeting I heard about recently. One of the men in the congregation rose and said, "This group knows me very well. I am sure that I have told lies; I have gotten drunk many times; I swear a lot; I gamble; I have even served time for stealing. But I will tell you one thing: sure, I've done all those things—but I have never lost my religion."

I want to reassure our speaker that I know this audience very well and that the people here tonight are every bit as good as that man—and some are even better. And I feel very happy about having a minister here, just in time!

In introducing the Reverend Mr. Blank, I do not know whether you will have questions for him when he finishes his speech, but it is often true that ministers ask the audience questions during a speech or a sermon. If that happens, I must warn you to be careful how you answer.

In that connection, I have in mind the minister who began his sermon one day by saying, "My subject today is 'Liars.' I think you will find that the 41st Chapter of Kings is highly pertinent. By the way, how many of you have read that part of the Bible?" About one-third of the people raised their hands.

"That's fine!" said the minister. "You are the people I am talking about. There is no 41st Chapter of Kings."

So be careful with your comments and your answers to any questions. Our speaker knows his Bible.

COLLEGE PRESIDENT

(The speaker is a college president or other high official.)

After giving the audience the speaker's background and just before presenting him, you may wish to insert the following:

I believe our speaker has been a university president long enough to join in the sentiments expressed by two former college presidents. They happened to meet by chance, years after each had resigned. One asked the other what he was doing now and the answer was, "I am in charge of an orphan asylum, and I enjoy it so much more than being president of the college; I never hear a word of criticism from a dissatisfied parent."

Said the other: "I am much happier too. I am now warden of a penitentiary—and I never hear a critical word from our alumni."

But our speaker seems to be a very happy person. I am convinced he likes it where he is.

CONTROVERSIAL SPEAKER

(The speaker is known as a controversial figure.)

If you are to introduce a person who you know is looked upon as a controversial figure—one against whom there might be substantial opposition among people in the audience—it is well to dampen possible animosity before it shows itself. The following can help in that kind of situation:

Our speaker tonight is a person who is sometimes referred to as "controversial." But, if you stop to think a minute, that word really means nothing except in terms of a particular kind of audience. Any one of us, no matter what our reputation, would be "controversial" if we were to appear before an audience made up of people who had been brought up with different beliefs. Just consider what a controversial figure George Washington would be if he appeared today before certain audiences. For instance, an audience of conservationists. He cut down a cherry tree! Or an audience of WCTU members. He kept the best cellar in Virginia! Or before an audience of Catholics and Lutherans. He was a Mason! Finally, he could not appear before isolationists because he made treaties with France and Poland and Germany that brought Lafayette and Koskiusko and Von Steuben to our aid; but he could not appear before the UN because he warned against entanging alliances!

Obviously, whether you are "controversial" or not depends on the make-up of your audience. And it is equally obvious that before this audience, which is made up of many kinds of people—all of us kind, understanding and sympathetic to a fault—nobody is really a controversial figure.

CROWDED ROOM

(Preliminary remarks when the room is crowded.)

When all seats are taken and people are standing along the walls it behooves the master of ceremonies to say a word about it:

I notice that people are standing in the aisles and I am very sorry about that. But I must add that I am also very glad about it. It is pleasing to all of us to have a speaker who draws a standing-room-only audience. In this connection I think I ought to tell you about the young science instructor who occasionally gave public talks on scientific subjects to make a few extra dollars. His subject was always abstruse and his audiences were without exception very small. Nevertheless, after every speech he made he would write home and tell his mother about how successful his talk was and how sincerely his audience applauded him.

One evening he was to make one of those highly technical speeches to a university audience, and about two hours before he was scheduled to speak a couple of students got hold of a truck, backed it up to the lecture hall, and carried out all the seats in the hall, loaded them on the truck and drove off. No one was aware of this until considerably later, when the audience began to gather for the lecture. It was then too late to do anything about it, and the rather sparse audience was forced to stand throughout his talk. But that evening when he wrote his customary letter to his mother, he said: "It was a tremendous success. I was given a standing ovation when I was introduced and another standing ovation when I finished. Not only that, but hours before I got there every seat in the house was taken."

When I see this overcrowded hall I am reminded of the man who met an old friend on the street and asked him how his wife was. The answer was: "My wife is in heaven." The other man, taken by surprise, said, "Oh, I'm so sorry," and then, remembering his friend's reference to heaven, said: "Oh, I mean I'm so glad." And then realizing that neither remark was very appropriate, put himself in an even worse position by saying, "Well, I'm surprised."

And so, looking over this packed room, I can only say that I am so sorry the room is overcrowded—but I'm so glad the room is overcrowded—or perhaps I just ought to say that I am surprised—but I'm happily surprised.

As I look over this crowded room I am reminded of what happened to the governor of a neighboring state. Soon after he was elected to office, he decided to visit the State Penitentiary. The warden, very pleased to have the governor calling on him and without warning the governor in advance, sent word to have all the prisoners gather in the huge dining room, where he then introduced his distinguished guest. The governor realized he had to say something but he was taken by surprise. He started out by saying: "Fellow citizens . . ." but it occurred to him that this was not correct. So he quickly added: "I mean fellow inmates . . ." But he then realized that this was not correct either—at least not up to that time. And so, after stammering a bit, he settled for: "Well, I am certainly happy to see so many of you here." And I'll settle for that, too—I am delighted to see so many of you here.

We realize that the room is too small for the number of people who wanted to be here tonight. We are very sorry for the inconvenience but we're also very glad to see so many people here.

This situation puts me in mind of the American pianist who was to give a concert in Paris. He received a cable saying that the theatre was sold out and they wondered if they could have permission to sell seats on the stage. His answering cable said, "Of course. And don't forget there should be room for three or four on the piano lid."

It is always pleasing to those who have had some responsibility for bringing out an audience and filling the hall to find that they have done too good a job and have overfilled it. On these occasions, I like to tell myself that the reason so many of you came out is that the advance publicity and the character of the program have drawn you irresistibly to this place. But on these occasions I cannot forget a little story I heard long ago which has always made me fear that there may be a less-flattering explanation for an overcrowded hall. At about 4:00 a.m., as an angry wife let her inebriated husband into the house, she said to him triumphantly, "So you have finally discovered that home is the best place after all." "Not exactly," said the husband, "What I found was that it's the only place open."

I give you that story in the belief—and certainly the hope—that it is absolutely inappropriate.

A speaker is, of course, always pleased to find that a standing-room-only audience has come to hear him. But those who are standing along the walls do not share his pleasure, and a speaker should take this into account. The following story helps:

I want you all to know that although it's always flattering to have a crowded house, I do not particularly enjoy seeing people standing in the aisles. In fact, seeing people lined up reminds many of us of the army days when you had to stand in line for anything and everything.

And that reminds me of the always unpopular sergeant who, in a rare moment of realization, said to one of the men under his command: "I suppose when you get out of the army, you'll be watching the obituaries for my death. And when it finally comes, you'll be delighted to spit on my grave!"

"No, sir," said the young soldier. "Once I get out of the army, I'm never going to stand in a long line again."

DEATH

(An important person connected with the meeting has died.)

It sometimes happens that after a meeting date and place have been set up, invitations or notices have gone out, and all preparations have been made, a person who has an important connection with the meeting dies suddenly. When that happens, there are usually some who insist that the meeting should be cancelled. This would admittedly be a gesture of respect for the deceased, but cancellation would, in many cases, involve great inconvenience to numbers of people who may already be en route to the city where the meeting is scheduled to take place or who may have cancelled other plans in order to be present. In addition, it is usually true that a majority of the people who are to attend the meeting have not been extremely close to the deceased person, and will take it as an indication of disregard for their convenience and their wishes if you do not proceed with the meeting.

It is obvious that a meeting under such circumstances cannot be introduced with a humorous anecdote. However, the occurrence does require a special introduction. The following lends itself to such a situation:

You are all aware that this meeting begins on a very sad note. John _____ was a good friend of many of us, and he was to have an important place in our proceedings today. His death was a shock to all of us, and I feel sure that my first reaction was also yours: we ought not to go on with the meeting without him. But all of us who knew

John best had a second reaction—and I hope you share this view with us: that the way to honor John the most is to proceed with this meeting as he would want us to do. We honor him far more by carrying out what he wanted carried out. His preference would never be for stopping progress, the progress he was helping to accomplish. He would consider cancellation of this meeting an empty gesture. So we decided—and I trust that you will concur in that decision—to do him the honor he would most appreciate: to go on with his work.

I do ask now that we all stand silently for a moment of thoughtful tribute to John _____.

(After a short silence:) Now let us proceed as he would want us to do.

DEFENSE AGAINST ATTACK

(You follow someone who has attacked your position.)

When your views have been attacked, it is best not to start at once with either a counterattack or an immediate defense of your position. If you give the impression of being angry or even greatly aroused by your opponent's attack, you make it seem much more formidable than you want your audience to believe it is. Your response should give the impression that you are relaxed and unruffled by what has been said, and for that purpose the following story is useful:

In responding to the previous speaker, I find, as I have always found in these situations, that if you look for points of agreement you find them, irrespective of how diverse your views may at first seem to be. Perhaps you have heard about the Protestant minister and the Catholic priest who were very close friends. One day they met on the street and, as always, they stopped to talk. On this occasion, the priest asked the minister, "How is your building fund coming along?" And the minister answered, "Very slowly. At this rate, we'll be waiting a long time for our new church. But I am still working to get donations, large and small, and we'll succeed somehow." Said the priest, "You know, we are old friends, and I wish I could make a contribution, but you can imagine the reaction of my bishop if I were to donate to the building of your new church." The minister said he understood that, of course, and they parted.

But the next morning the minister found in the mail a letter from the priest with a very sizable check enclosed. The letter said, "I have been thinking the matter over, and it occurred to me that you are going to have to tear down the old church when you build your new one, and I know that costs a lot of money, so my check is enclosed. My bishop will be delighted to hear that I have contributed to tearing down your church."

Bearing in mind that if you search for points of agreement you find them, let me point out. . . .

If your opponent's argument leads you to believe that it may have been too abstruse or too complicated for the audience to understand, or if you would like to take the tack that your opponent's position is simply not understandable, you might want to say:

When I consider what my friend has just argued, I can only say that it reminds me of the young lady who snuggled up to her escort and said, "How about giving me a diamond bracelet?" The answer ran something like this: "The insoluble difficulty confronting me is that extenuating circumstances preclude my purchasing a bauble of such extravagance." And the girl said, "I don't get it."

And her escort answered, "That's what I said—you don't get it."

And in this case, I must say that extenuating circumstances also preclude me from comprehending what the gentleman has said—I just don't get it.

DEGREES, OVEREMPHASIZED

(You are introduced with overemphasis on your college degrees.)

There are occasions when a chairman or toastmaster is eager to impress the audience with your credentials. Often, a general audience momentarily resents a speaker whose Master's and Doctor's degrees are being flaunted. To avoid that reaction, the following is helpful:

Your chairman has given you not just my name, which would have satisfied me, but has generously gone into some detail about some of those initials that people often put after my name. If I ever had any pride in those, I lost it when I heard the following anecdote:

A gentleman motoring in the East decided to have a look at Williams College. He came upon an institution consisting of several buildings on what appeared to be a beautiful campus, and he said to the first man he met, "Is this Williams College?" The man replied, "No, this is the State Insane Asylum." The visitor was somewhat embarrased by that, and he said, "Oh, I'm sorry. This place really looks a lot like Williams College." But the other man answered, "Well, they're not alike at all—to get out of here you have to show improvement."

Ever since I heard that story I have been a little self-conscious about those degrees.

◆◆◆◆◆

I appreciate your chairman's very complimentary introduction. He included a reference to my college degrees, and I have to tell him that although I used to be very proud about such references, I heard a little story recently that somewhat changed my attitude.

It seems that a young fellow just out of college applied for a position at a pharmacy, and the proprietor, in outlining the young man's duties, said to him, "The first thing you need to do every morning is sweep up." The young man was appalled. He said, "But I am a college graduate!" And the pharmacist answered, "Oh, that's all right—I'll show you how."

DELAY

(The speaker's late appearance delays the meeting.)

Sometimes the chairman receives a message to the effect that the speaker will arrive late; his plane is delayed or some other happening prevents his arriving on time. It is well on those occasions to inform the audience promptly; otherwise they may become restive or the vacant chair may cause them to doubt that the speaker is going to appear at all. After stating that there will be some delay and describing its cause, the following story may be used to mollify your hearers a bit:

Of course, in a sense, our speaker is not late at all. You may remember the little tale of the boy who was playing marbles with a package under his arm. As dusk began to fall, and he continued playing, a neighbor who happened to be passing by said to him, "Shouldn't you be getting home? Aren't you going to be late for dinner?" The boy answered, "I'm not going to be late—I've got the meat."

Our speaker will be here soon and he's bringing the meat.

When the speaker of the evening has been delayed, you need to fill the gap in the program as well as you can. In addition, the audience needs reassuring that the speaker is on his way, and in telling them so you might add:

I don't happen to know the cause of the delay, but the speaker is a very well known and distinguished person. That fact reminds me of a little story. An internationally known film star was taken suddenly ill in an eastern city. It was decided that she should leave the theater immediately and be flown to a hospital in New York, where specialists awaited her arrival. So, she was bundled up in her sables and driven to the airport, but for almost an hour she was not allowed to board the plane. Finally, one of the specialists phoned the airport to ask what was causing the delay, and an airport attendant explained: "It is the wind," he said; "the wind is blowing so hard here that we simply haven't been able to lay down the red carpet."

Considering the reputation of our speaker, I can well imagine that this could be the explanation for his delay, too.

The failure of a guest speaker to arrive well in advance of the time for his introduction to the audience creates an extremely difficult situation for the chairman. The latter must take pains to show no distress or embarrassment, and he can do that best by way of an anecdote such as the following:

I must tell you that our speaker has not yet arrived. We have tried to reach him without success and I assume that he is on his way and will soon be with us.

The situation reminds me of the lady who appeared in court to obtain a divorce. After some questioning, the judge said to her, "I have been listening for some time to your testimony about your husband and it seems to me that your only complaint is a very slight one. Are you seriously trying to get a divorce on the ground that your husband has been careless about his appearance?"

And the lady answered, "Yes, your honor; he hasn't appeared in over a year!"

I really don't believe that our speaker was careless about his appearance here today. And I feel sure that he will be with us in much less than a year. But I do ask your indulgence for a few minutes.

As soon as I have any further word for you, I shall report it.

If an when the speaker appears, he should of course be introduced at once.

If more than a few minutes elapse without further word from him, the chairman ought to fill the void in one of two ways. One way is to pick up a few items of the organization's business that might otherwise have waited for another meeting; this focuses the attention of the audience on something other than the speaker's absence.

Another way is to throw open to discussion by the membership of the audience, the subject that was assigned to the missing speaker. It may be necessary for the chairman to introduce that discussion with his own views, briefly stated. This activity not only serves to divert the attention of the audience from the chairman's difficulty, but also gives them something to do—in a way which leads into the speaker's presentation if he does appear.

DOCTOR

(You are to introduce a physician.)

In introducing the speaker of the evening, I remember a story that the late Senator Paul Douglas, who was a Ph.D., used to tell on himself. His doorbell rang one evening, and the maid answered it. There was a woman at the door who said, "My husband is not feeling well, and I know Dr. Douglas lives here. Could he come over and see my husband?" The maid answered, "You're making a mistake. Mr. Douglas has a doctor's degree but he's not the kind of doctor who does anybody any good."

Our speaker, as you know, is an M.D.—the kind of doctor who does people good. I hope you will not misunderstand that statement. I don't mean that he "does" people when he sends his bills: I really mean he does people good.

◆—◆—◆—◆

I know that people expect a chairman to be reminded of stories and anecdotes that are clearly indentifiable with the speakers they are introducing. I am departing from that custom in order to tell you the following very short story which you will agree immediately does not in any way refer to the physician, Doctor Blank, whom I am introducing:

Recently the president of a hospital made an announcement. He said, "The Board of Directors has decided that we should add another operating room. This in turn will probably involve a new Mortuary and Post Mortem room."

I am sure that I need not tell you that our speaker is not in any way connected with that hospital.

I do wonder, however, whether he is the subject of a little verse I came across recently. Somebody reacted to a news item that reported that doctors spend an average of 18 minutes with a patient. The comment on that item was in verse as follows:

> In eighteen minutes all is done,
> Including diagnosis,
> And writing a prescription out,
> And cautioning on doses.
> That's minutes in consultation,
> But no one, I assume,
> Has figured all the hours
> Spent in the waiting room.

I must now present him at once—or he will be complaining that I have kept him waiting!

DRESS, UNSUITABLE

(Your clothing is unsuitable for the occasion.)

Sometimes "black tie optional" is interpreted by a speaker to mean that he need not wear his tux. Then, when he arrives at the affair, he finds that practically everybody at the speaker's table is in fine sartorial array and he is in a business suit. Or he has decided in favor of "dressing up" only to find that he is practically the only person at the speaker's table who is not in a business suit.

In either case, an anecdote serves to relieve embarrassment for everybody, especially the speaker himself. Under such circumstances, he could tell the audience—

As you can plainly see, my friends at this table and I were not quite unanimous in our choice of attire this evening. I was at a loss to know whether, being so full of my subject, I should wear full dress, or whether, because I want to be businesslike about my subject, I should wear a business suit. As you notice, I apparently made the wrong choice.

It puts me in mind of the army officer, a colonel, who, when off duty, was occasionally guilty of highly reprehensible conduct. And speaking of suits, as I am—on one occasion the military police arrested him because, in an inebriated condition, he was chasing through a hotel hallway in his birthday suit with a beautiful damsel fleeing from him. His commanding officer, a general, was very fond of the colonel and always went out of his way to get him out of scrapes. He was hard put to it in this case, but he finally was able to report to the colonel that the charges had been dismissed. The colonel later discovered that his acquittal was due to the fact that the general, in reporting the incident, referred to a provision in the Military Rule Book which said, "It is not compulsory that an officer wear a uniform at all times, so long as he is suitably garbed for the sport in which he is engaged."

I hope your chairman will be able to dig up some special provision in the etiquette rule book which will excuse this evening's indiscretion on my part—so that I might, shall I say, "re-dress" my crime.

EXAGGERATION

(Your opponent exaggerates or makes extreme statements.)

When countering an opponent's exaggerations, it is not enough merely to say that they are overstatements; nor is it ever advisable, of course, to accuse your opponent of lying. But the following anecdote may well serve to make the audience doubt his statements and at the same time give them a smile:

Some of Mr. _____'s statements strike me as rather extreme, to say the least. In fact, they put me in mind of the farmer whose house was situated at the foot of a very steep hill. A visitor remarked that it was too bad that the hill was too steep for plowing. The farmer replied, "Not at all. At the end of winter, the ice melts and the big rocks come rolling down the hill and they plow the land." The visitor then said, "Well, but you certainly can't plant anything on that hill." The farmer replied, "Sure I can. Planting is easy. I just stand on my front porch and shoot the seed out of my gun in even rows up and down the hill." The astounded visitor said, "Is that the truth?" The farmer answered, "Hell no! I'm just trying to make our conversation interesting!"

I've decided that Mr. _____ is just trying to make our debate interesting.

F

FLATTERY

(You have been introduced too flatteringly.)

When the chairman has been extremely generous in his remarks about you it is best to tell the audience in some jocular way that the chairman has exaggerated. To do so is usually wise for several reasons. It dispels the thought on the part of the audience that you too think very highly of yourself. In addition, it gives the audience a more intimate glimpse of you than they can get from the more formal part of your speech. Finally, it diminishes the great expectations that may have been aroused in the audience by the introduction, and helps to reduce them to a level which hopefully you will exceed.

Any of the following stories will serve the purpose:

I have been listening with great interest to your chairman's introduction. Until he finally reached my name I sat there wishing I could be half as qualified a person as the stranger he was describing; I was sure those beautiful phrases could not possibly be intended to describe me. Now that I find that I am actually the person he thought he was describing, I cannot help but wonder whether the chairman was not the central figure in *this* little story: After listening to a number of fish stories told around the circle of men at the Fishermen's Club, they turned to a man who had thus far said nothing and asked him whether he had caught anything that day that was worth mentioning. He thought a moment and then said, "No, nothing worth mentioning That last one I caught was too small to take home, so two men helped me throw it back in the lake."

◆—◆—◆—◆—◆

I very much appreciate your chairman's complimentary remarks. They were so much more enjoyable than introductions which are sometimes inadvertently given. For instance, I was to talk to a church group and as I entered, I saw that the bulletin board said: "The title of the sermon today: Do You Know What Hell Is? Come In and Hear _____ [your name]."

◆—◆—◆—◆

I want to thank your chairman for those highly complimentary words. I want to assure him also that I only hope he believes what he said—because I don't.

I determined long ago that I would not let flattering introductions go to my head, and in order to prevent that, I learned a bit of verse. Right now I feel the need of reciting it to keep down the conceit which your chairman has engendered in me. So here it is:

> If you get to heaven
> You will likely view
> Many folks whose presence there
> Will be a shock to you.
> But just keep very quiet;
> Do not even stare.
> Doubtless there'll be many folks
> Surprised to see you there.

I think now I'm back to normal, and we can concentrate on the subject of the evening.

Your chairman has certainly been very kind to me. Whenever I am introduced in such complimentary terms I think back on that little verse that says:

> Whenever I get compliments
> I do as most folks do;
> I get a bit embarrassed,
> But I don't deny they're true.

I appreciate all the fine things your chairman has said about me. My response runs like this:

> Oh, how we blush when thanked or praised,
> And say, "There's nothing to it.
> Don't mention it." And yet just see
> How disappointed we would be
> If people didn't do it.

The chairman has been very kind in his introduction of me. I can only hope that he meant everything he said.

I have in mind the case of an East Indian who came to the United States and asked a young man with whom he had served in the Army whether he would give him a letter of testimonial to help him find employment. The young American promptly sat down at his desk and wrote a testimonial letter, which the East Indian read and found extremely flattering. However, as he went around looking for a job, he found that the interviews went reasonably well until he handed over the letter of reference. That always ended the interview without his getting the job.

After a few such experiences he asked someone if there was some connection between this flattering letter and his not being employed. The letter read:

"I would gladly recommend this man to my mother-in-law, my landlord, my first sergeant, and to every second lieutenant in the United States Army."

I can only hope that I am not missing some hidden meaning in your chairman's very flattering words.

I have been listening to the very complimentary introduction your chairman has given me. I am sorry to say that it reminds me of a cartoon I saw a few days ago, in which a father is saying to his little boy, "And there, my son, you have the story of World War II," and the little boy is answering, "But daddy, why did they need all those other Marines?"

I just hope that after hearing that flattering introduction you won't ask me some question of that kind.

That flattering introduction puts me in mind of the patient who had just completed psychoanalysis. The doctor said to him, "This was your final session with me. You are cured. How do you feel about it?" And the patient answered, "Some cure! Before I started coming to you, I was Napoleon; now, I'm nobody!"

Of course, I feel just the opposite. Before I came here today, I was nobody. After that introduction, I feel just like Napoleon!

When I hear such a highly complimentary introduction, I am always afraid it will make me conceited. But I guess it is much too late to think about that.

I do try to remember a word of advice I heard long ago: "Swallow your pride. It is non-fattening, and it will make you grow."

I enjoyed all the complimentary remarks that your chairman was kind enough to make. His introduction was quite different from one I experienced some time ago in an elevator on my way up to the meeting place. A young man got into the elevator with me and on the way up he said, "Are you going up to the meeting?" I said that I was. He said, "They've got some speaker on the program. It won't be any good." I said, "No, it will probably be un-interesting." He said, "Yeah, but I have to go." I said, "Yes, I have to go too."

When we got off the elevator we separated, and I didn't see my friend again until I was leaving and, with a number of other people, he got into the elevator with me. I waited expectantly for some complimentary remark. What he said was, "Well, we were right, weren't we?"

If the chairman's introduction includes complimentary remarks about your speechmaking ability, you may wish to respond in this way:

Your chairman has made very kind remarks about my speechmaking ability. I would enjoy those remarks much more if I didn't remember the public speaking instructor who followed the example of Demosthenes and required his pupils to begin practicing public speaking by putting marbles in their mouths. They began with six marbles and he permitted them to reduce that number by one each day. Finally, they reached the day when he said to them, "Now that you have lost all your marbles, you can begin speaking in public."

I can only hope that the chairman was not making a hidden reference to that story.

FOREIGN AUDIENCE

(You are to speak before an audience of foreign visitors.)

Whenever you are to speak before an audience that is predominantly of a nationality different from yours, the problem of creating a bridge between you and the audience is accentuated. A humorous anecdote that is pertinent always helps to build that bridge. For instance:

I am aware, of course, as you are, that I am of a different nationality from most of you. I consider that this makes not the slightest difference. I think people the world over, of whatever nationality or color or creed, basically have the same difficulties and problems and the same hopes and goals. So in the broader sense, we speak the same language and we need no interpreter. And that reminds me that on one occasion when the president of the United States was addressing a Chinese audience, a native Chinese was selected to interpret a few sentences at a time to the audience. During his talk, the president told a joke that took him about five minutes. The interpreter listened to it throughout, then spoke in Chinese for only a few seconds, and the audience roared with laughter, which pleased the president very much.

When he had finished his speech, the president said privately to the interpreter, "I was interested in the fact that you could tell that joke in Chinese in about one-tenth of the time it took for me to tell it in English." Said the interpreter, "Mr. President, I didn't think it was very funny. So I said to the audience, 'The president has just told a joke; please laugh heartily.' "

Thanks for *your* laughter! I'm very pleased that you responded that way without any urging from an interpreter. That just proves what I was saying—that we don't need one.

FOREIGN SPEAKER

(You are to introduce someone from a foreign country.)

Introducing a foreign visitor to this country often presents special problems. The perfect introduction would not only influence the audience to listen sympathetically to whatever he might say, but would also make him feel welcome. The following story helps in both those directions:

Three or four of my collegues and I often eat lunch together at a nearby restaurant. We sometimes have very spirited discussions and arguments, and the proprietor, who arrived here some years ago from Greece, frequently comes to our table and listens with obvious interest, but without saying anything.

These have usually been gripe sessions—we gripe about hard work, long hours, high prices, dishonest politicians, and generally air our various dissatisfactions. Not one of those topics ever caused the proprietor to utter a single word until one day, after all those months of silence on his part, he suddenly joined in and, in a loud voice and with profanity, he blasted hard work, long hours, high prices, dishonest politicians—all in one outburst. We were astonished, and someone said to him, "What has happened to you? You have never said a word all this time, but now you are protesting as loudly as any of us." With a satisfied smile, the proprietor took from his pocket a certificate which he proudly exhibited. "Yesterday," he said, "I became a U.S. citizen!"

I realize that our guest did not come to this country to become our fellow-citizen, though it may be our loss that he does not intend to do so. But I want him to know that he is free to comment and criticize and find fault—in other words, to join us just as though he were our countryman.

It is always well to create a tie between a foreign speaker you are introducing and the audience. On such an occasion, the following will be found useful:

As you know, Mr. _____ is visiting us from his native country, _____. Not only is he most welcome here this evening, but it is undoubtedly true also that he and we have much in common. I know beyond a doubt that we have at least one thing in common—and it is perhaps best illustrated by this story:

The board of directors of a civic organization was discussing a project which some members of the board were anxious to embark upon, despite the fact that everybody recognized that doing so might put the organization "in the red." Finally, one board member—a substantial donor to the organization—who was opposed to the project rose and said, "Just remember this: I never remain a member of any organization that knowingly goes into a deficit."

That created a serious silence, until one of the other board members asked, "Do you mean you're not going to remain an American citizen!"

These days it is difficult to find a country that is not operating out of a deficit balance. I would guess, therefore, that in addition to many other things, the speaker and we surely have that in common.

FUND-RAISING

(Your speech deals with raising funds.)

Calling upon your audience to make a contribution or donation requires a combination of delicacy and backbone. You have to make it very clear that you are indeed looking to them to pay out money, but you have to do so in a way that does not subject them to embarrassment.

The right combination of those elements is often to be found in an appropriate anecdote. It can be very pointed, and yet because it is only a story and produces a smile it does not offend. There are many fitting examples:

I am hopeful that you will make a contribution to our organization. Considering the fine purposes to which your money is put, I am never bashful about asking for it. I am not like the young man who wrote to his rich uncle, asking him for money. At the end of the letter he put a P.S. which said: "I am sorry to be asking you for money. After writing this letter I was so embarrassed that I even ran after the messenger who was mailing the letter for me, but I was unable to catch him." He soon received his uncle's reply. It, too, had a P.S. attached to it which read: "You don't have to be at all embarrassed. Your letter never reached me."

Unlike that young man, I am asking for money in a good cause.

I know you are familiar with the saying that the Lord loveth a cheerful giver. We hope you are one—but we have no restrictions. We take money from old grouches, too.

And we have noticed that grouches feel so much better after they have given, that, having donated, they automatically qualify as cheerful givers.

I often direct my appeal for funds to the women in the audience. That's the result of my hearing about the husband who shouted to his wife, "That son of ours has taken money out of my pocket." His wife tried to pacify him. "How do you know our son did that? I might have done it." But her husband answered, "No, no. You didn't do it—there was some left!"

So I want to encourage the wives present to exhaust that source of donations.

I hope my appeal to you for funds will be as successful as Bishop Sheen's was on one occasion. A family in very moderate circumstances was so moved by him that they proceeded to round up all the money in the house, and altogether they were able to produce a total of $5.35. When some question arose as to whether they should give all of that to Bishop Sheen, the mother of the family said, "We are going to give it. It will come back to us manyfold." And they did.

About a week later the family won a hundred-dollar bond at a drawing at the supermarket. And when they discussed what they ought to do with $100, the six-year-old son promptly answered, "Let's put it all back on Bishop Sheen."

I can't promise you that kind of return in money, but I can promise you a feeling of great satisfaction and the knowledge that you are contributing to a most worthy cause.

I have a friend who has the faculty of making small things sound important. For example, he owned a Japanese camera that was not in very good condition, and when he finally succeeded in selling it he reported to me that he had disposed of a portion of his foreign holdings. On another occasion when he gave someone four quarters for a dollar, he turned to me and said, "I enjoy taking part in a currency exchange program."

Tonight I am asking for a donation to our organization. If my friend were present he would put it much more delicately. He would say that there should be a reshuffling of proprietary interests. I know, because when his car was repossessed, he described it with that phrase.

The donation forms are now being distributed. I hope you will favorably consider my recommendation that we have a reshuffling of our proprietary interests.

We would, of course, like to have your check this evening, but if it is more convenient for you to give us your pledge tonight and pay later in the year, that would please us almost as much.

Perhaps you remember the story of the hold-up man who went into a Chinese restaurant and passed a note to the cashier which said: "Wrap up all your money!" The cashier read the note and then said, "Oh—to take out?"

We don't need your money to "take out." Your pledge for payment later will make us very happy.

If you don't happen to have your checkbook with you, we will be just as happy if you give us your pledge and pay later. You may recall the salesman who in the course of his sales pitch realized that his prospective buyer was unable to pay cash, so he said to her, "Madam, you pay a small deposit and then you pay not another dollar for six months." And she said, "Who's been telling you about us?" We haven't heard a single derogatory word about you. We're only suggesting the pledge as an alternative if you would prefer to contribute that way.

We do, of course, want your financial help, but I hope you notice that we ask for it in a subdued voice and with a very mild manner. I have heard about a gentleman who in the process of raising funds for his organization came upon a prospect who he had been told in advance had plenty of money but was very stingy about making contributions. And when he began to doubt that he was going to get any money at all from this man, he finally said to him in desperation: "If you don't give us a contribution we're going to tell all the other organizations that you did."

If you decide to make a donation to our organization your name will go down in our list of contributors, and that is indeed a Roll of Honor. You may remember that when a visitor to a new concert hall called the Mann Auditorium remarked to the mayor that he thought it was very commendable that the mayor had named the hall after Thomas Mann, the mayor corrected him. He said, 'No, we named it after Frederick Mann." "Well," said the visitor, "I know, of course, what Thomas Mann wrote, but what did Frederick Mann ever write?" Said the mayor, "A check."

So even if you have not written a single book, just writing a check can bring you gratitude and recognition.

In connection with the possibility of your making a contribution to our organization, let me remind you of the young Hollywood starlet who was asked why she broke her engagement to a very wealthy friend. Her answer was, "One day I saw him in a swim suit and he looked so different to me without his wallet."

I like the looks of all of you—but I must confess that if you were to take out your wallets I would consider you far handsomer.

I must correct an advance announcement that you may have seen concerning this meeting. One sentence in it contained a typographical error. It said: "We hope you will participate with us in the many functions of the organization." We meant to say: "We hope you will participate with us in the money functions of our organization."

It is always difficult to decide how much to give to an organization. Let me try to help you solve that problem. I suggest that each of you make out a check for $500. Now let me explain. A century ago, a member of the Fire Brigade in Springfield went to the office of a lawyer by the name of Abraham Lincoln and asked him for a contribution. When the man had finished his appeal Lincoln said, "I'm going to give you $20. Tonight I'm going to tell my wife that you wanted $50 for the Fire Brigade, and she will say, 'Abe, I hope you have more sense than that! $20 is quite enough.' And so," Lincoln added, "you come around tomorrow and get your $20."

I am suggesting $500 so that all of you can report to your spouses that you were asked for $500 but you had more sense than that, and all you did was make out a check for . . . whatever amount you now decide.

◆—◆—◆—◆—◆

I realize that it is very difficult to decide on the amount you feel you ought to give. In doing so please remember the conversation the late rich Texan, Paul Getty, had with the reporter who was interviewing him. The reporter asked, "Is it true, Mr. Getty, that if you added all your investments, your securities, your real estate—all your assets—the total would amount to a billion dollars?" Getty thought for a moment and then he said, "Well, I suppose it would, but you must remember that a billion dollars doesn't go as far as it used to."

Confidentially, our assets add up to less than a billion—and please remember that less than a billion dollars doesn't go as far as it used to, either.

◆—◆—◆—◆—◆

In the past we've been very gentle in our fund raising. We mention it in a subdued voice, and we never embarrass anyone. I now recall, however, that a committee whose duty it was to raise a church fund called upon a man who said, "I can't give you any money at all; I owe too many people now." "Well," said one of the fund raisers, "Don't you think you owe the Lord something, too?" And the answer was, "I suppose I do, but he just isn't pushing me like my other creditors."

So tonight, consider us as pushing, just like any other creditor.

◆—◆—◆—◆—◆

It's always difficult to decide how much to give, and I would not presume to decide that question for you. However, I can give you a test question for you to answer to yourself: After you have decided how much you are going to give, ask yourself this—if you were on trial accused of being generous, would there be enough evidence to convict you?

When you give to our organization—considering its motives, its purposes and its results—you never regret it. Nobody has ever changed his mind and stopped payment on a check he gave to us. Perhaps you remember the doctor who called up his patient and said, "Your check came back." And the patient said, "Yes. So did my arthritis."

In our case if you want to be cured of that uneasy feeling that you are not doing enough, just send us a check and that feeling will never come back—unless of course, your check does.

I know there are other demands on your money, and I know that you are the only one who can decide how much you want to distribute to which recipients. You cannot dodge the question like the husband who was awakened in the middle of the night by his wife, who whispered to him, "There's a thief going through your trouser pockets." And the answer was, "Well, you're just going to have to fight it out between you."

I know that there are some especially modest people here who like to make a donation privately, without any publicity about it. I admire that, of course. I don't mind their being shy—just so they're not shy the money. However, I don't want them to handle it the way Mark Twain handled it on one occasion. He handed over a check in a sizable amount and the solicitor tried to hand it back to him, saying, "Mr. Clemens, you forgot to sign the check." And Mark Twain answered, "On no, I want to make this gift anonymously."

We are happy to accept anonymous gifts, but you will understand that we have to know to whom to send the receipt.

◆—◆—◆—◆

We are hoping that on due consideration you will honor us with a generous check. And if you would like to split your contribution into several installments we will be just as pleased to receive several checks through the year. However, please understand that we do not intend to handle those checks the way George Bernard Shaw liked to have his checks handled. On one occasion Shaw was in his living room conversing with a guest when the plumber, who had been repairing the water pipes in Shaw's home, interrupted to say that he had finished the job. Shaw then asked him what the amount of his bill was, and upon being told, said: "Very well. I assume you want it in several small checks as usual." And he sat down at his desk and made out four checks, which he then turned over to the plumber.

When Shaw rejoined his guest the latter said, "It is really none of my business, but if you don't mind my asking—why do you pay the plumber in four checks instead of one?" And Shaw replied, "Because the plumber can sell those checks at a much higher price to people who save autographs." And then Shaw added, "And I rather like the arrangement because, you see, those checks never get cashed."

You must not be under any misapprehensions. No matter how you split it up, we're going to cash your checks.

Some people are very sensitive about making a fund-raising speech, but I am not one of those. I ask and plead and beg and implore. Not only that, but I am never embarrassed by the response I get, as long as it's accompanied by a contribution. No matter how resentful or impatient or angry people may get, I take it. In that respect, I am like Norman Vincent Peale.

He said that on one occasion he pressed a very rich man, a potential giver, so hard that the man finally took out a thick wallet, pulled out a handful of bills and threw it at him. In reporting the incident to his Board, the Rev. Dr. Peale said, "I picked up $600 before I realized I had been insulted."

I am therefore ready to expect any kind of retaliation with any kind of contribution.

You may recall that a restaurant owner one morning put up a sign reading, "Don't insult our waitresses by offering them tips." And one of the waitresses promptly set up a little box on the counter, marked "Deposit Insults Here."

In my case, however, to make sure they will reach me, if you have any insults just write them right on your checks.

I am sure it is no secret to this audience that we are in a fund-raising campaign—and that means *you* are in a fund-raising campaign. I was tempted to follow the example of a very wise minister who once announced to his congregation, "I have prepared three sermons for this morning. What I call my Ten-Dollar Sermon lasts one full hour. My Fifty-Dollar Sermon lasts twenty-five minutes. My One-Hundred-Dollar Sermon lasts only five minutes. Now we will pass the collection plate and see which sermon I deliver."

Instead, I am going to trust you. I can see from the generous expressions on your faces that you will do nothing to deserve a full hour's speech. I shall talk to you, therefore, for only a few minutes—but, of course, I take for granted that the size of your contributions will be in inverse proportion to the length of the speech.

In connection with my purpose here tonight, I must tell you about the man who knocked on his neighbor's door and when Mrs. O'Flaherty opened it, said, "I am very sorry to bother you, but I hope you will contribute something to the Home for Alcoholics." And Mrs. O'Flaherty answered, "If you will come back about eleven o'clock tonight, I will be glad to. You can have Mr. O'Flaherty."

I want to make sure that, although we want contributions, that kind would not be acceptable. We ask that you restrict your donations to cash, money orders, checks, stocks and bonds—any of those and preferably all of those!

Like you, our organization has discovered this year that money disappears faster than ever. It has put us in mind of the professor who had built up a reputation over the years for being the most absent-minded professor of all time. Two of his neighbors were talking about him and one said to the other, "Did you hear what Professor Baker did yesterday? He gave his wife some money to take to the bank and as she left, instead of kissing her, he kissed the money good-bye." Whereupon the other neighbor said after thinking a moment, "You know—the professor is not as absent-minded as I thought he was!"

We are not absent-minded at all, but we are thoroughly aware—and I am sure you are too—that these days you no sooner receive a donation than you realize you have to kiss it good-bye.

In speaking to a group of people who are to constitute a committee of fund-raisers, you might wish to talk to them along the following lines:

I know I don't need to remind you to be sure to express your thanks and the thanks of our organization to every donor without fail. However, I must caution you to be careful in voicing your appreciation so that you will not inadvertently displease some contributor.

I have in mind the case of the American colonel who was stationed in London during the war, and while there, regularly worshipped at a certain church until it was destroyed by an enemy bomb.

Promptly after the war, the parishioners proceeded to raise funds for its restoration, and remembering the colonel, they wrote to him asking him if he would like to contribute. He responded handsomely, sending them his check for $5,000. And they, in turn, expressed their gratitude by sending him a record of the remarks made at a church meeting after receipt of his generous donation.

But on playing the record and hearing the very first remark reproduced on it, the colonel, in a fit of temper, threw it on the floor and stamped on it. That first remark was, "Let us begin by thanking the colonel for this timely succor."

I hope you will remember in obtaining contributions that the more people you contact the more money you will raise. So oi course we want you to call on people, write to people, telephone people—the more the merrier.

However, please remember the salesman who said to a brother salesman, "I made some very valuable contacts today."

The reply from that other salesman was: "Yes, I didn't make any sales today either."

So please remember that although we want contacts, those are not enough. We need sales, and in our terms that means contributions, memberships and dues.

However, I do owe you one more story in this connection:

A young woman driving her car along the highway was stopped by a police officer for speeding. When he looked at her driver's license he said: "Your license shows that you need glasses in order to drive safely, so you are certainly going to get a ticket."

Said the lady: "Officer, I have contacts."

Said the officer: "Lady, I don't care if you are the mayor's sister—you are going to get a ticket."

So you see, he didn't consider contacts enough, and neither do we.

◆━◆━◆━◆

It occasionally happens, especially when the audience has already paid rather heavily for the dinner at which you are speaking on behalf of your organization, that you do not want to press for the payment of any more money from your audience, and yet you would like to have them contribute at a later date. In that case, you might use the following:

I have told you about the aims and purposes of our organization and I hope you will keep them in mind in the future, even though I am not asking that you donate tonight any more than you have already contributed to this event.

However, I do want to remind you of the man who went to his psychiatrist complaining that his memory was very bad. "In fact," he said to the psychiatrist, "I forget everything right away. What do you suggest I do?"

Without a moment's hesitation, the psychiatrist answered, "Pay me in advance!"

So, of course, if there is any chance at all of your forgetting, then give us your check right now. But if your memory is reasonably good, we trust you—at least for a week.

Sometimes your audience will consist so largely of people who have already made donations of recent date to your organization that you feel it unwise to make a "pitch" for more money; yet you are reluctant to let the opportunity pass for reminding them of the financial needs of your group. In that case you might use the following:

I am aware—and indeed grateful—that most of you have fairly recently made a contribution to the organization. We thank you for that. Of course I do not want you to forget us for too long. Just remember the boy who went to college and, after a few months, wrote his parents, saying:

"Dear mom and dad, I haven't heard from you in nearly a month. Please send a check so I'll know you are all right."

By all means remember that, from time to time, we just want to know that you are all right.

I am reminded of the conversation which was overheard at a restaurant recently.

Sitting at the table were a young, light-haired and also light-headed young woman and a very elderly gentleman. He said: 'I'm much too old for you."

Said she: "Goodness, no, George! Three million dollars isn't too old."

And three million dollars isn't too much, either—but we'll take less if you say we must.

At annual meetings called for the purpose of obtaining pledges, an appeal is often made to members of the audience to raise the amount they pledged the previous year. The following is appropriate for such appeals:

In this connection, I think I ought to tell you about what happened at an annual fund-raising meeting of a charitable organization a couple of years ago. In the audience was a man whom no one had ever seen before at those meetings. When the speaker called for pledges from the audience, a considerable number of people responded, pledging ten thousand, five thousand, fifteen thousand, etc. Finally, the unknown man stood up and asked, "What is the largest amount that anybody has ever pledged to this organization?" The reply was "$100,000." Said the man, "I pledge $125,000." This was exciting news, and there was great applause and much patting on the back as this gentleman's pledge card, duly signed, was handed to the speaker.

When two or three months had passed with no word from this donor, it was decided that a small committee would call on him and find out about payment. He greeted the committee at his office, and in response to their very polite inquiry, he answered, "I'm not paying." When the committee pressed him for his reasons, he said merely, "Business is not quite as good as it was; and anyhow, I've changed my mind."

The committee was irate and shortly thereafter the organization filed suit to collect the pledge. There followed the taking of depositions, the trial of the case, the entry of judgment for the full amount, garnishments, levies on real estate, attachments, and every other applicable legal remedy. The pledge had been made in January; by December 31, the organization had finally succeeded in collecting the full amount of $125,000.

But now it was January again, and there was the usual meeting with its appeals for pledges. In walked the man who had made the largest pledge in the history of the organization. Of course, this time everybody purposely avoided him. The last speaker made an eloquent appeal for funds, describing the crucial needs of the organization, and ended with a plea to those who had pledged the previous year to raise their pledges for the coming year. At this point, the uninvited guest rose and made this statement: "I have been much moved," he said, "by the speeches this evening. I did not realize how great the needs of the organization really were. You have asked us to raise our pledges of last year, and I am ready to do that. Last year I pledged $125,000; this year, I pledge $125,000 and court costs."

You might like to close your appeal for funds with something along the following lines:

We would, of course, welcome any contribution you might wish to make right now, but if you would prefer to put the pledge card in your pocket and think it over, by all means do so. In fact, I like to think that the more consideration you give your donation, the more considerate you will be—and we are quite willing, of course, to rely upon your kindness. You may remember how one man was describing to another how very kind his uncle was. "My uncle," he said, "is one of the kindest men I have ever met. Of course it's true that although he is a very rich man, he never sends me or any of his other nephews and nieces any money at all; but he is very kind." And the other man said, "And you call that kindness?" "Yes, indeed," was the response. "That's what is called unremitting kindness."

You understand, of course, that we are definitely not asking for your unremitting kindness. We want you to check any impulse to be unremitting; in fact, the larger the check the better.

A minister on one of the T.V. gospel programs ended his broadcast by reading from letters written to him by listeners. Each letter mentioned that the writer was enclosing a contribution, and told the dollar amount of the check being sent. Then, in closing the program, after some complimentary remarks about the contributors, the minister looked straight into the camera and said, "And now, my dear funds . . ."

In addressing fellow alumni and urging them to contribute to their alma mater, you may want to give them your version of the Latin origins of the word "alumnus." Your version is that the first syllable "alum" comes from the chemical term "alum" and, as everybody knows, "alum" is a strong drying agent. And, the second syllable "nus" comes from the Latin verb "nutrire" meaning to feed or to give. It is obvious, therefore, that an alumnus who lives up to his name keeps on feeding his alma mater and giving until he is dry.

If donations to your organization are income tax deductible, you will of course stress this point in seeking contributions, and the following story is appropriate:

On that matter of tax deductibility, you may be interested in hearing about an incident that occurred in connection with another organization, which like ourselves is tax exempt. The president of the organization received a phone call one day from an Internal Revenue Service agent, who said, "Mr. John Blank has shown in his current income tax return that he made a donation to your organization in the amount of $5,000. We are just checking to find out if you have received that donation."

And the answer was: "No, we have not. BUT, WE WILL!"

In addressing members of your organization, you are going to be raising funds, obtaining new members, etc. You will, of course, prepare them for the fact that they will encounter opposition of various kinds. You will encourage them not to be too easily dissuaded, to persevere, to try to be more persuasive. But you will concede that there are some people who simply cannot be persuaded. In that connection, the following story is appropriate:

Perhaps you have heard about the very wealthy man who received a delegation from a charitable organization and who, after listening at some length to their pitch, finally said, "Gentlemen, my father has, for many years, had a serious case of arthritis and is unable to work. My sister's husband left her and she actually scrubs floors to support herself and her five children. My brother has been in the hospital for the last few months. And if I have never given a dime to help any of them, what makes you think I would be interested in donating to your organization?"

It is often true that women are the most successful fund-raisers, either because they are willing to give more time to that activity or because they feel more deeply about their duty to their organization. In any case, it is often worthwhile to appeal directly to the women in the audience to make telephone calls, to write letters, etc. In that connection you might wish to use the following item:

I am making this special appeal to the ladies to raise funds because I know they have a special expertise in that department. Ask any husband!

Also I recall overhearing a conversation between two women at a restaurant table near mine. One woman said to the other, "I'm sure you know that there are those among your friends who believe that you married your husband because he was very well to do."

And the other woman responded: "Well, I didn't really want to marry him for his money. It's just that there was no other way of getting it."

I hope that all the ladies present will remember that—and that you will get the money, one way or another.

GENERATION GAP

(Preliminary remarks when your audience is either elderly or young.)

When you find that your audience includes a considerable number of people either older or younger than you are, you might wish to say an introductory word or two to bridge the gap. For that purpose, consider the following:

I notice that there is a considerable age difference between many people in this audience and myself. We used to call that a generation gap, but I have decided that these days there is almost no such thing. Today it is very largely true that the young are almost as sophisticated as the elderly, and so the gap is narrowing all the time. Consider the case of the eight-year-old who came home one snowy day without his new sled. When his parents asked him where his sled was, he said, "Oh, a man and his little boy borrowed it and they're going to bring it back to me here at five o'clock."

His parents were naturally disturbed, but they decided to say nothing and to let events take their course. They felt that when nobody showed up with the sled, the boy would learn a valuable lesson.

To their surprise, promptly at five o'clock the doorbell rang and there stood a man with his little boy and the sled—and a candy bar, to boot. The eight-year-old took the sled and the candy bar, ran back to his bedroom and in a moment returned. He then examined the sled, and finding it still in excellent condition, said to the little boy, "OK, now you can have your watch back."

This incident has helped me to realize that the width of the generation gap is grossly exaggerated.

That there is a generation gap is of course not at all surprising. I am sure that our grandparents were shocked or at least surprised at some of the things our parents did; and that our parents were shocked or at least surprised at some of the things we did; and so why should we not be shocked or at least surprised occasionally—just as our children will be. It all grows out of a difference in point of view. For example, I have a business acquaintance whose name is Harry. When the phone rang the other day in his home and his wife answered, a voice asked to speak to Harry. The wife said, "Do you mean Big Harry or Little Harry?" There was a moment's hesitation and then the voice answered, "I guess it's Big Harry—the one in fourth grade."

So it all depends on where you sit—on the point from which you are viewing life. And I am sure we are all eager to hear the point of view of our next speaker, Mr. Blank.

Like you, I hear a great deal about the generation gap. But sometimes it seems to me that there is no gap at all—that it has already been jumped by the youngsters, and that they have joined the oldsters in many ways For instance, the other day a first-grader walking down the hall in school slipped and sprained his ankle. A teacher standing nearby picked him up and said to him, "Remember, Johnny, big boys don't cry." Nothing was farther from Johnny's mind. "Cry!" he said. "Are you kidding? I'm going to sue."

With an appropriate reference to the age of the audience, whether the audience is primarily elderly or young, the following stories will bring laughter:

Many years ago, a speaker who was on the program with President Eliot of Harvard University referred to the university in glowing terms and, among other things, called it "a storehouse of knowledge."

When President Eliot was called upon, he said, "Let me tell you why Harvard is indeed a storehouse of knowledge. It is because the freshmen bring in so much knowledge when they come, and the seniors take away so little when they leave."

I think this audience ought to be reminded that in some respects there is indeed a wide gap between generations. When a newspaper recently ran an article about nursing homes for the elderly including pictures of some of the rooms with furnishings, etc., not a single comment was received from readers.

But when a Chicago newspaper ran an article on student life at Yale and showed rooms and furnishings at a fraternity house, there were numerous communications from the public. The mayor of a nearby city demanded the return of a sign that had been stolen from the front of his store and that was clearly depicted in one of the photographs. A steamboat line wanted two life preservers shown in one of the pictures returned at once. Standard Oil demanded the return of an Exxon globe hanging from the ceiling of a dormitory room.

You can plainly see that there's a very great difference in the way the new generation furnishes its quarters.

There is also a great difference, as I am sure you are aware, in the amount of direction and compulsion that is acceptable to the older generation and unacceptable to the newer generation. The latest instance that has come to my attention involved a father who, as his son walked out of the front door one evening, called, "Have a good time!" The boy was half out of the door but he promptly turned and, facing his father, said angrily, "Don't tell me what to do."

If you wish to make the point that there is no great gap between the generations, you might like to use the following:

A group of people were standing at the curb waiting for the light to turn green when a man in the crowd, disgusted with the appearance of a young person standing in front of him, said to an adult waiting at his side: "Look at that one! You can't tell whether that is a boy or a girl."

The person he addressed answered very sharply: "It's a girl. I happen to know because she is my daughter."

Of course, the man was embarrassed at that. He said immediately, "Oh, I apologize, madam. I would never have said that if I had known you were her mother."

And, of course, the answer was: "I'm not. I'm her father."

HUNGRY AUDIENCE

(You are asked to speak first, as dinner is delayed.)

Rather than permit the audience to become restive because the meal is delayed, it is best to start the program even if it must be interrupted later by the arrival of food. Under such circumstances you may be called upon to deliver your speech while the audience is waiting. You might begin by saying:

I am very sorry that I am not a cook or even a caterer. If I were, I assure you that I would not be serving you merely with food for thought—but at the moment that's the best offer you have.

I am reminded of Chauncey Depew who, as you may know, gained a national reputation as an after-dinner speaker. Perhaps I can work up a reputation as a before-dinner speaker. Incidentally, on one occasion Mr. Depew was introduced by a chairman who said, "Chauncy Depew can always produce a speech. All you have to do is give him his dinner, and up comes his speech." And when Depew began his talk, he said, "I only hope that it isn't true that if I give you my speech, up will come your dinner."

◆—◆—◆—◆

Or, if you prefer:

I believe your chairman must have asked me to fill this void with a speech believing that I might say grace at such length that upon its completion, the dinner would arrive. But I wouldn't do that to you. The grace I have in mind is very short. I say only, "Bless this meal—when and if it arrives—and the tender hands that are now unfreezing it."

Or, perhaps:

I have occasionally been called upon to take the place of a scheduled speaker who was late in arriving, but I have never before taken the place of a dinner that was late in arriving.

This situation puts me in mind of Daniel in the lions' den. As one of the lions came toward Daniel, Daniel was relieved to see that the lion stopped a couple of feet away from him and assumed a prayerful attitude, looking toward heaven with his paws crossed in front of him. A moment later, the lion advanced toward Daniel, who said to him, "I am very glad to see that you are a religious lion and therefore I assume you are not going to eat me." But the lion answered, "On the contrary, Daniel—I was just saying grace."

Of course, on this occasion, I am not saying grace at this time because grace is usually a way of giving thanks for the food set before us. At this moment it would be rather foolish to give thanks for the food set before us; I am, however, praying that it soon will be.

Everything has its good side—even this delay. The longer we wait, the hungrier we all get and the better the dinner will taste when it comes.

I understand that the menu of a cafe in Chicago shows two vegetarian dinners. One is listed at $2.00 and the other at $1.50. The difference is that the higher-priced one doesn't have spinach.

Perhaps when this dinner comes, it will happily turn out to be the higher priced one.

This delay reminds me that a maternity shop received a note from a customer which read, "After weeks of delay, you have finally delivered that maternity dress I ordered. I am returning it to you with this note. My delivery was faster than yours."

I hope that you will like my delivery. Apparently your chairman decided that my delivery would be faster than the hotel's.

It is always somewhat difficult for the speaker when the chairman decides that the program should be speeded up because the dinner is being delayed and the audience may become restive.

Since it is not easy to satisfy the audience's appetite with a speech instead of a meal, you might like to put your hearers in good spirits with one of the following:

I think this is the first time that I have ever been served up to an audience in lieu of food, but I'll do my best.

This delay in the service puts me in mind of the man who picked up the telephone in his hotel room and asked for room service. When he was connected with the hotel kitchen he gave his order like this: He said, "I'd like half a grapefruit—but don't take the seeds out; and don't cut it into segments. Just leave it as it is, seeds and all. Then I want two boiled eggs—one boiled for 2-1/2 minutes and the other for 9-1/2 minutes. Toast—charred black on one side, but hardly touched on the other side. Coffee—not very hot; just lukewarm. Cream for the coffee—just turning sour." Then he said, "Now, may I have that in about ten or fifteen minutes?"

The voice from the kitchen answered "Fifteen minutes! I can't get that up to you in less than an hour and a half. That's a special order!"

Whereupon the man answered, "Special order? That can't be. Yesterday I ordered grapefruit, eggs, toast, and coffee with cream—and that's the way I got it as a regular order!"

I assume—and I hope—that the delay tonight is caused by special orders, not by regular orders.

We are very sorry for the delay. We believe it will be ended momentarily. Meanwhile, we can suggest only that you have another drink. And in that connection I want to remind the ladies present of the man who said to his lady friend: "You know, drinking makes you look beautiful!" Said she, "But I have not been drinking." Said he, "I know, but I have."

So my word of advice to the ladies is to encourage your escort to pass the time by having another drink— which will make you look increasingly beautiful—while we proceed to speed up the service.

I am sure that you would rather eat than listen, but at the moment you don't have a choice. However, we have checked, and we are assured that we will have dinner very soon.

We have been checking because we thought the hotel chef might be catching up on his sleep just like a fellow we remember, the father of small children who was catching up on his sleep on the living room couch. The sleeper's children were playing rather noisily in the same room. In fact, they were hoping to arouse their father so that he would join them. But he lay there motionless even when their noise awakened him.

Finally, the most agressive of the youngsters climbed up on the couch and pried open one of his father's eyelids, but his father purposely did not move.

Whereupon the child turned to his brothers and sisters and said, "Well, I can tell you this much: he is in there all right."

I can now give you that same reassurance about the chef. He is in there and we expect to be eating any time now.

ILLOGICAL ARGUMENT

(You want to attack your opponent's logic.)

Sometimes the most effective way of opposing an illogical argument is to poke fun at it. For that purpose, the following anecdotes are useful:

I have listened very carefully to my friend's argument, and it seems to me that his logic leaves something to be desired. As a matter of fact, it puts me in mind of the lady who had made a number of donations to an animal shelter, and decided that she wanted a cat. Naturally, she went to that shelter and picked out her cat. A few days later, she brought the cat back and said, "You have to take it back. This cat is a bird killer. I simply cannot stand an animal that kills birds." Then she added, "However, I shall, of course, still make donations to this shelter. In fact, as soon as my husband comes back from his trip, I'll get a check from him. He's up north, shooting ducks." Somehow, my friend's logic reminded me of that story.

Or you may prefer:

When I listen to Mr. _____'s logic, I'm reminded of the Irishman who said, "I wish I knew where I will be when I die!" Someone asked "Why? What good would that do you?" And the answer was: "Well, don't you see—if I knew that, I would just never go there!"

◆━◆━◆━◆━◆

I listened carefully to the argument just made, and I think the logic of it—or rather the illogic of it—needs examination. Listening to that argument, I was reminded of the speech made by someone who told his audience that he had tried brandy and water one evening, then gin and water the next evening, and then whiskey and water the third evening, and each evening after his drinks he found he was highly intoxicated. From these experiences, he told his audience that it was obvious that water was a highly intoxicating drink, since no matter what you mixed it with, it made you drunk.

◆━◆━◆━◆━◆

I have listened with care, as you have, to the facts presented by my friend and also to his conclusions from those facts. And that combination of facts and conclusions reminded me of the speaker who was promoting prohibition. The speaker had before him two glasses and a can of worms. He dropped a couple of worms into one of the glasses and then filled the glass with water. The worms were unaffected. He then put a couple of worms into the other glass and filled that glass with whiskey, and the worms promptly shriveled and died. Said the speaker, "You saw what happened. The lesson is obvious." And then with his eyes fixed on an elderly man in the front row, he said, "And what is that lesson?" Said the man, without a moment's hesitation, "The lesson is if you have worms, drink whiskey."

◆━◆━◆━◆━◆

The gentleman's logic is just a bit faulty. His conclusion only *seems* logical. It is like the conclusion that a speaker reached as a result of a survey taken recently at two universities—Yale and Vassar. The report of the survey showed that Yale graduates had 1.3 children and that Vassar graduates had 1.8 children. The conclusion drawn from that survey was that it proved that women have more children than men.

The logic of the gentleman who has just spoken reminds me of the barber who was trying to sell his customer on getting not just a haircut but also a singe. When the customer rejected the idea, the barber said, "You're making a bad mistake. Cutting the hair causes it to sort of leak out; its energy goes out the cut end; then the hair gets weaker and it falls out."

Said the customer, "Listen—I shave every morning. I've done that for thirty years and my beard is stronger than ever. How do you answer that?"

And the barber replied, "That's easy. You are just not the fellow that story was made up to tell to."

I guess I'm just not the fellow my friend's argument should be told to.

When the speaker takes an arbitrary position clearly based on bias without reference to logic, you might want to say, in a good-natured way:

Our speaker tonight reminds me of a certain Southern bus driver on a sight-seeing bus. His job was not only to drive the bus but also to announce to his passengers the points of interest on the drive. He would point to a vacant field and say, "On your left is the site of a Civil War battle. A handful of our Southern boys routed 10,000 Yankees."

Next he would point out a plot of ground, saying, "That's where one fine battalion from Georgia annihilated a whole corps of Yankee troops." Finally, he went further than some of his Northern passengers could stand. He said, "Here's where two brave Virginia boys captured an entire regiment of Yankees."

At that, one of his passengers said with a broad New England accent, "Didn't the North win a single victory during the entire war."

The guide answered, "No, Ma'am, and the North isn't going to win one as long as I drive this bus."

When someone, in presenting an opposing view, is guilty of false logic, after you point out the illogicality, you may want to add:

That kind of argument puts me in mind of the fellow who went into a restaurant and ordered pizza. When it arrived, he said to the waiter, "Would you be good enough to cut it into slices for me?" And the waiter said, "Of course, I'll cut it into eight slices." At which the man exclaimed, "Oh, no, I could never eat eight slices of that! Cut it into six slices."

I have listened carefully to my opponent's presentation and I can only say that he reminds me of a student I happen to know. This student flunked four courses and barely passed the fifth one with a D. Naturally, he was called in by the Dean, who sat him down and asked him, "How did you happen to get four F's?" Said the student, "Well, I guess that was my mistake. I think I neglected those four courses and I spent altogether too much time on that other subject I got a D in."

Of course, I don't know what other subject my opponent has been spending time on, but I really don't think it was this one.

◆◆◆◆◆

I have been listening to my friend's argument and I must say that I find it not only unconvincing but confusing to boot. In fact, his argument reminded me of the lady who attended a League of Women Voters meeting because the speaker's topic was "International Trade" and she was eager to learn more about that subject. Afterward she confided to a friend: "I've always been so confused about international trade, and that's why I went out of my way to attend the meeting today. Now, I'm still terribly confused—but on a much higher plane!"

◆◆◆◆◆

I find myself in disagreement with the previous speaker. I think his facts are incorrect. I think his conclusions are quite wrong. I think his logic doesn't stand up. Otherwise, I like this presentation very much!

You notice I don't accuse him of untruths. I think he is telling the truth as he sees it—but that he sees it wrongly.

This all reminds me of the train that used to run between two small towns in Wyoming. One of those towns was Eurelia—E-U-R-E-L-I-A. When the train was approaching Eurelia, one of the conductors would open the front door and call out: "You're a liah!" Then the conductor at the other end of the train would open the door and call out: "You really ah . . . You really ah."

Those conductors were not really accusing anybody of telling an untruth. And I want to reassure my friend on the other side of the platform: I know you as an honest man—out a mistaken one as I see it. You really ah. You really ah.

IMPROMPTU SPEECHES

(You are called upon to speak without prior notice.)

I am sure you all agree with me that the human brain is a wondrous thing. I have always known that the brain starts working the moment you are born. But I have now found out that it stops working the moment you are called on to speak in public.

◆━◆━◆━◆

Your chairman has suddenly decided to call on me for a few words. I should have been spending this minute and a half (that has elapsed since I knew I was to be called on) by thinking up a fine, clear, logical statement. Instead, I have been spending that time wondering why the chairman has called on me, and I have now recalled an incident which explains this:

A football team had been playing a very poor game practically all the afternoon, kicking poorly, missing passes, fumbling. Late in the game, a substitute, at a nod from the coach, began running up and down in front of the bench to warm up. After a couple of minutes of that, the coach threw a football to him, and he dropped it. And then someone in the stands called out, "OK—you can send him in. He's ready."

I think that explains the situation. Your chairman looked us all over and decided that I was ready.

INSULTS OR INVECTIVE

(Your opponent makes insulting remarks about you.)

When an opponent indulges in insults, you are very tempted to answer him in kind. Be assured, beyond any doubt, that you run a far greater risk of losing your audience by uttering insults in return than you do by handling the whole matter casually and, if possible, humorously. That treatment often results in the audience's resenting, in your place, what your opponent has been saying; and it also indicates to the audience that what he has been saying is without basis—or how could you take it so lightly? An appropriate story helps:

What you and I have just been listening to puts me in mind of a little story. When John Steinbeck was at the height of his popularity as an author, he was often invited to sit at the speaker's table at important meetings. On one of those occasions, at a dinner meeting at a New York hotel, the chef, who happened to be a great admirer of Steinbeck's, prepared a cake in the form of a bus. This was at a time when Steinbeck's *The Wayward Bus* was at the height of its popularity. When it came time for the dessert, a waiter walked across the dining room carrying aloft a reproduction of "The Wayward Bus" with the words clearly marked in frosting on its side for all to see. It was, of course, brought up to the speaker's table and placed in front of Steinbeck, who promptly cut a large wedge of it for himself and began to consume it to the great enjoyment of the audience. The toastmaster immediately took a microphone and said to the audience, "This is a wonderful occasion; this is the first time that I have ever seen a speaker eat his words."

I believe, as we go along tonight, that I may be able to make this the second such occasion.

A farmer driving a team of mules arrived home much later than usual. His wife took him to task for it and he then explained his tardiness. He said, "I had to pick up the preacher, and after he got on, my mules didn't understand a word I said."

If my friend had gone a little farther in calling names and making insulting remarks, nobody would have understood him except mules.

Now let's get back to the issues. After all, those are what you came to hear.

My friendly opponent, who has just told you in a few choice words what he thinks of me, puts me in mind of a little story.

A navy captain was addressing his men aboard ship. The ship's wireless operator came on deck with a message he had just received from the admiral. He said in a low voice to the captain, "I have a message for you from the admiral, which he asked be delivered at once." The captain answered, "Oh, a message from the admiral! Read it aloud." The wireless operator suggested that the captain read it for himself, but the captain said, "Oh, no, read it aloud."

Accordingly, the wireless operator read aloud this message: "Of all the blundering, stupid, idiotic morons I have ever known, you take the prize." Without batting an eye, the captain said, "Very well; have that decoded at once and bring me the message. It may be important."

I want you all to know that I'm having my opponent's remarks about me decoded, and I feel sure they will turn out to be interesting—but I doubt that they will turn out to be at all important.

My friend has chosen to talk about me instead of about the subject assigned to us. As interested as I am in the many complimentary remarks he has made about me, I think it is regrettable that he does not tell us all more about what we are here to discuss tonight. He reminds me a little of something that happened during the Lincoln-Douglas debates. On one occasion, Douglas made some remarks about Lincoln that were as derogatory—and also as irrelevant—as my friend's remarks about me this evening. In answering, Lincoln said that he was reminded of a very small and very old steamboat which plied the river during his boyhood. He said that the boat was so dilapidated that when the whistle was blowing, the paddlewheel would stop, and when the paddlewheel was going, the whistle wouldn't work. Said Lincoln: "Douglas reminds me of that old steamboat, because apparently when he is thinking, he can't talk, and when I hear him talk, I realize he isn't thinking."

I am not going to spend any time telling you about my opponent; I am going to spend my time thinking and speaking on the subject before us.

As I listened to the gentleman who has just spoken, it seemed to me that he would have made more mileage with you people if he had done more talking about the subject we are here to discuss and less talking about me. As it is, he has put me in mind of a courtroom situation I heard about recently. An attorney and his lady client were sitting on one side of the table, and on the other side sat her opponent and two lawyers representing him. As the trial went on, the lady finally turned to her lawyer and said: "I think we are at a great disadvantage. When one of those lawyers is talking, the other is thinking, but when you are talking, nobody is thinking."

I have tried not to fall into that trap. While my opponent has been talking, one of us has been thinking.

The gentleman with whom I am sharing the platform this evening has made a few rather uncomplimentary remarks. They put me in mind of an incident that occurred in World War II. A whole platoon of our men was hauling heavy ammunition cases on a hot sunny beach, on a boiling hot, sunny afternoon. And lying in the shade of the palm trees was a group of natives, doing nothing except watching the soldiers.

One of our men, as he was picking up one of those heavy ammunition cases, said under his breath, "Damn ignorant fools!" One of his fellows promptly said to him, "Why say that? You don't even know them." And the answer was, "Oh, I don't mean them, I mean us!"

In the same way, I feel sure that when my friend was saying those angry words, he meant *him*—not me!

On those occasions when an opposing speaker resorts to wild statements and becomes overexcited, it is always best not to follow any such lead, but on the contrary, to remain calm and unruffled. On such an occasion, you may want to tell the audience:

My friend's excitement and heat and his language might have made more of an impression on me if I hadn't heard about the church janitor who was sweeping the floor after a fiery sermon by the preacher. Among other things, the janitor swept up pages of the preacher's text, and he was surprised to read a notation in the margin, next to a particularly exaggerated statement. The notation said, "Argument here weak—talk very loud."

My friend on the opposite side of this platform has let his tongue carry him a little bit too far. Fortunately, I don't mind too much. It may relieve his feelings somewhat, but it does his cause no good.

Perhaps a little story will help him keep his temper; at least it's worth trying for your sake if not for his.

A young man was shopping in a supermarket with his baby propped up among his groceries in his cart, and the baby was screaming at the top of his voice or yelling— whichever is louder. And as the young man pushed his cart through the aisles he was heard to say: "Don't get excited, Albert . . . don't yell, Albert . . . don't scream, Albert."

One of the other shoppers approached the young man and said to him, "I must say that you are certainly to be commended for trying to soothe your little son, Albert." Said the young man, "Lady, I am Albert."

You may prefer to deal with your opponent's attacks on you with a short aside such as the following:

I have, on occasion, spoken very well of the gentleman. I have sometimes complimented him highly. That makes me doubly sorry that he speaks so ill of me. But, after all, it's possible that both of us are mistaken.

INTERRUPTION

(An incident in the hall interrupts your speech.)

Sometimes the interruption takes the form of angry insistence by someone in the hall that he be allowed to take over the meeting. Though this is a rare occurrence, when it does happen it is embarrassing to the chairman and is usually difficult to handle.

On such occasions, the chairman must keep always in mind that he needs the support of the main body of the audience against the intruder or his group. Therefore, the chairman must keep as placid an exterior as possible, keeping his voice level, maintaining his patience and continuing to treat the intruders far more politely than they deserve.

At the outset of this kind of interruption, a joke or anecdote is out of place. The chairman must resolutely state that the intruders are out of order, that they will not be heard except upon recognition by the chairman and then only for a short statement of their position. He or she must gavel down the opposition, if necessary, ignore their attempts to be heard and proceed with the business of the meeting.

Such interruptions are far more easily handled if the chairman has a loudspeaker at the rostrum and there is no loudspeaker available to anyone in the audience. With such an arrangement, the chairman will find it much easier to down opposition and proceed with the business of the meeting.

If the interruption gets completely out of hand and there is physical contact on the floor, the chairman should immediately deputize someone to call the police, but he should not, under any circumstances, leave his position at the podium as chairman of the meeting.

When order has been restored, and the meeting can proceed in order, a story or anecdote is once more appropriate, and indeed very welcome. For that purpose, the chairman might consider something along the following lines:

> I am always slow to do anything about someone who misbehaves in an audience because of an experience I had some long time ago. There was a noisy person in the audience who was annoying the people around him and generally interrupting the proceedings, and I rebuked him and shouted him down. Later, I found out he was an idiot. I resolved never to make that mistake again.

LEAVING OFFICE

(The speaker is leaving office.)

When an officer of an organization completes his term and does not stand for reelection, or is transferred to another city or for some other reason is going out of office, it often happens that a luncheon or dinner is given in his honor. On such an occasion complimentary speeches are made, and they tend to follow a pattern. A speaker who pays the retiring officer compliments in a somewhat different way is often the one most appreciated. However, under those circumstances it is important that any anecdote which in any way refers to the retiring officer, whether serious or funny, be laudatory. For example:

We are deeply indebted to John Blank for his dedicated service to this organization. Finding a person to take his place is going to be extremely difficult. Perhaps you remember the office executive who had the task of filling the position of an officer who was about to retire. This executive had never forgotten that he was a Yale graduate. The advertisement he ran read this way: "Wanted for executive position, a Harvard or Dartmouth graduate—or a Yale man for half-time."

It is just the other way with us. I think to fill John Blank's shoes we need two Yale men ready to work overtime."

◆—◆—◆—◆—◆

Finding a person who can adequately fill the void that will be left by John Blank is difficult indeed. You may remember that when John Jay was sent by General Washington to be Ambassador to France after Benjamin Franklin had been our French Ambassador for several years, Jay was greeted by a French diplomat who welcomed him and said, "We have already been informed that you are going to replace Mr. Franklin." But John Jay replied, "Then you have been misinformed. I have come to succeed Benjamin Franklin. No one could replace him."

In connection with John Blank's record of accomplishment with us I must tell you about the young woman who was telephoning a record store, and her finger slipped and instead of the record store she reached a wrong number. She was of course unaware of this, and when a man answered she said, "I just want to ask you if you have "Eyes of Blue."" He was somewhat taken aback, but he recovered himself and said, "No—but I have got a wonderful wife and four sets of twins." Still thinking she had the record shop, she asked, "Is that a record?" And his answer was, "I really don't know, but I never heard of anybody doing better."

Now I don't know whether you can consider John's employment with us a record, but I am sure you will all agree that nobody could have done better.

I am sure that your estimate of John Blank's value to this organization is no different from mine. Perhaps I can best tell you how I feel about John's record with us by relating a little story having to do with the great composer, Igor Stravinsky. Some years ago, when Billy Rose was producing Broadway hits, he obtained Stravinsky's consent to the use of one of his compositions in one of Rose's productions.

After the first night's performance Rose sent a cable to Stravinsky saying: "Your music was a colossal success. However, I would like to substitute three saxophones for the woodwinds. I believe it would be an even greater success. What do you say?"

Rose promptly received an answering cable from Stravinsky which said merely: "Satisfied with colossal success."

I have no doubt that the applicants for John's position will be telling me they can do the job better than he has done it. But I just want to tell John that I'm satisfied with colossal success.

LONG SPEECHES

(Preliminary remarks regarding the length of your talk.)

I have been cautioned by your chairman not to overstay my time. I shall be careful about that. I remember that on one occasion at a luncheon meeting I inquired of the chairman how long he thought I ought to talk. His answer was, "You can just talk as long as you want. However, we'll all be leaving at two o'clock."

◆—◆—◆—◆

The following serves the same purpose:

I shall be careful to stay within the time allotted to me. I'll never forget the occasion when an elderly gentleman who was, we might say, in his "anecdotage," held a friend of mine on a street corner talking to him far too long. Finally the old man said, "I'm afraid I've been boring you," and my friend answered, "Not at all; I haven't been listening."

I'll try not to talk *that* long.

You may want to preface your speech with introductory remarks along the following lines:

I want to assure you that I shall not make a long speech. It may, of course, seem long, but if you check your watch—or, perhaps, the calendar!—you will find that it is well within bounds. I promise not to forget about the woman who phoned the television editor of one of the newspapers and asked, "How did that show last night finally end? I want to know because it was definitely the most interesting and delightful show I have ever seen on T.V. and I have to know how it ended."

Naturally, the T.V. editor asked, "How did you happen to miss the end of it?" And the lady answered: "I fell asleep."

I realize that no matter how devastatingly smart or clever I may be, if I talk too long, you will fall asleep anyhow.

I remember hearing about the minister who was preparing the first sermon he was to give to his new congregation. He prepared it very carefully and then decided to test it out by taping it and then listening to see how it sounded. He found out. The silence at the end of the tape woke him up. He had fallen asleep about halfway through it.

No, I didn't tape this talk. But I am thoroughly forewarned by that minister's experience.

MEETING YOUR OPPOSITION

(You are in partial agreement; you are in wide disagreement; your opponent is oversimplifying; your opponent is exaggerating, etc.)

When you find you are in wide disagreement with another speaker, it is best to give your audience an early warning of the fact that you will be arguing along quite a different line. In doing so, it is never wise to ridicule your opponent or to cast aspersions on his position. It is far better to make a quiet point of the fact that you and the other speaker are apparently a considerable distance apart; and for that purpose the following is useful:

> A young lady who had been going with a young man for a considerable time was asked by a close friend how they were getting along. She hesitated and then, with some stammering, said, "Well, right now we are having a slight dispute. You see, I want a big wedding and he wants to break the engagement."
>
> I think that's a fairly close analogy to my differences with the gentleman who has just spoken. We are in the same kind of slight dispute.

◆━━◆━━◆━━◆

It often happens that someone on a discussion panel with you or in an actual debate with you is guilty of exaggeration. On such occasions, you will find an appropriate story more effective than your accusation that your opponent is exaggerating. You might say, for example:

I wonder if my friend is not overstating his case. In fact, as I listened to him, he reminded me of a letter I read long ago that was addressed by a young man to his girl friend. It read: "I would climb the highest mountain to be in your company. I would swim through a torrent just to see you for a moment. I can hardly wait for Wednesday evening to come so that I can be with you again." He signed it, and then he added a P.S.: "If it rains Wednesday, let's make it Thursday."

These days, speakers often refer to "semantics." Frequently, in a panel discussion, someone will remark that there is no substantial difference between his view and someone else's—that it is just a matter of semantics.

If you find yourself in a position where you wish to show that there is a much wider divergence of view than can be attributed to the use of words, you will find the following useful in pointing out how important semantics can be:

The previous speaker has been trying to assure you that there is no fundamental difference between his view and mine—that only a matter of semantics is involved. Well, semantics often prove to be of importance. What appears to be a mere difference in wording often turns out to be a basic difference in view. We should all remember the plight of the young man who was looking very disconsolate, and a friend said to him, "What's the trouble, John, you seem very discouraged." John said, "I certainly am. The girl I've been going with for years just told me that she'd be faithful to the end." "Well," said his friend, "I should think you'd be delighted to hear that." Said John, "You don't understand. She's going to be faithful to the end. I'm the quarterback."

Semantics, you see, can be enormously important.

Especially when your opponent has made remarks that are vague or illogical, you may find the following useful:

My friend on the other side of the table reminds me of Senator Green, who, you may remember, was in active life even after his 90th birthday. One day at a Washington cocktail party, he was discovered looking surreptitiously into a little notebook he had taken out of his pocket.

Someone asked him how many parties he was supposed to attend that day. "Five," he said. The other person then said, "And I suppose you were looking to see where you were going from here."

"No," said Senator Green, "I was trying to find out where I am now."

At first I thought my opponent was trying to figure out where his argument was going from here; but after listening for a while, I have decided he was only trying to find out where he is now.

MICROPHONE FAILURE

(The speaker has to shout to be heard.)

All too frequently, a speaker finds that the microphone does not work properly. Until it is fixed, he needs to talk very loudly. This is troublesome to the audience and the speaker alike, and to allay his hearers' impatience and at the same time prove his own equanimity under such circumstances, the following is appropriate:

I realize that because of this troublesome microphone it may be difficult for people in the rear of the room to hear me. I shall try to talk loudly enough to be heard by everyone in the room. This puts me in mind of the speaker who, when his microphone went dead in the middle of his speech, asked if everyone could hear him. Whereupon a man sitting in the second row rose, turned to the rear of the room and said, "I can still hear him clearly. If somebody is sitting where you can't hear a word, I'll be glad to trade seats with you."

With that in mind, I don't dare ask whether you all still hear me—but I'll keep on trying to be heard, anyhow.

NAME, MISTAKEN

(You are introduced by the wrong name.)

It occasionally happens that a chairman, particularly one who must introduce a number of speakers, will make a mistake in a name—or forget it entirely. The writer, in fact, still remembers an occasion of many years ago when the chairman told at length of a speaker's background and career and then, at the moment of introduction, was actually unable to come up with his name. It was an embarrassing moment not only for the person being introduced, but for the chairman and the audience as well. At first extremely flustered, but then regaining his composure, the chairman said, "I hope this is one of those times when I may be permitted to say 'This speaker needs no introduction' "—and he took his seat.

It happens much more frequently that the introducer inadvertently furnishes the wrong first name, or omits a syllable in a long last name, and on any such occasion, the speaker might make the correction and at the same time amuse the audience with the following:

Names are often difficult and I suppose mine is no exception. It makes no great difference but I might remind the chairman that my name is really _____. In this connection, my mind goes back to something that happened to President Theodore Roosevelt. He was always very proud of remembering people's names, and he very much disliked ever having to admit that he had forgotten one. One evening after he had made a speech, people lined up to shake hands with him. In that line was the man who made the President's shirts. And since the President had not ordered any shirts for some months, the man was curious to see whether the President would remember his name. As they shook hands, the man said, "Mr. President, I don't know whether you remember me—I made your shirts." And the President replied, "Why, Major, of course I remember you!"

When the chairman or toastmaster introduces you to the audience by the wrong name it is always embarrassing to him. One way of relieving the situation is to show that you are taking it lightly, realizing that it could happen to anyone. You might, therefore, go on to say:

> I want to reassure the chairman that this is not the first time that my name has been misstated or misspelled. I am used to it—and immune to it. I do not react at all the way a well-known author reacted to printers' errors. They occurred so often in his books that he said that when he died he would like to have this epitaph cut in the headstone at his grave:
>
> > I have suffered so much from printers' errors
> > That death for me can hold no terrors.
> > No doubt this stone has been misdated.
> > Oh, how I wish I had been cremated.
>
> I don't feel that way at all. I hope your chairman will forget all about it as promptly as I will.

It sometimes happens that in introducing a speaker the chairman confuses him with someone else and wrongly states his name.

In responding to the erroneous introduction, whether the audience has noted the error or not, the speaker ought to make the correction—but he ought to do so as gently as he can. Either of the following stories will serve in that connection:

> Your chairman has introduced me under another name. I happen to be George K. Henderson—but I hope your chairman will realize his slip of the tongue has done no harm whatever. In fact if the FBI has been looking for me, that introduction may throw them off the track.
>
> Actually, the only harm he has done is to remind me of a story. A businessman of my acquaintance had made an appointment to meet officers of the Allis-Chalmers Corporation at their office in Wisconsin. A few days prior to that appointment he called his secretary into his office and in a great hurry he said to her, "Write to Allis-Chalmers and say that I cannot keep our appointment Friday because I'm off for Texas in a hurry. I'll phone when I get back. Sign my name."
>
> When he returned to his office a few days later, he read the carbon copy of his secretary's letter. It said: "Dear Alice: Can't keep our date," etc.
>
> My friend grabbed the telephone and called one of the officers of the Allis-Chalmers Corporation. When he had him on the wire, he said, "I hope you haven't read a certain letter!" But the answer was, "Read it! It's been on our bulletin board for three days."
>
> I want to assure your chairman that his slight slip-up will not be publicized in any way.

> I'm sure you all remember the famous true story of the general in World War II who, when the enemy demanded his surrender at Bastogne, sent back a message, "Nuts!" That was Major General McAuliffe. After the war he was often called upon for a speech and, without fail, the person who introduced him always retold that

story about McAuliffe's one-word message. And he not only grew tired of hearing it; he came to hate it—because he felt that, when people told that story, it was as if they considered that his contribution to the war was that word, "Nuts!" instead of the four hard-fought battles in each of which he had a major role.

But one evening when he was introduced as the speaker, he realized that, at last, there had been no mention of his famous message, and he was delighted. He was delighted, that is, until he finished his speech and the chairman rose and said, "Thank you, General McNuts!"

I told that story because I wanted your chairman to hear that awful mix-up by another chairman so that he will feel very good about his own very slight slip-up.

It does occasionally happen that, through a failure in the preparations, or a last minute substitution, you are introduced by the wrong name. You feel the necessity of correcting the mistake but you must do so in a very light, and, if possible, humorous vein.

Here is a very short anecdote to use in correcting a mis-introduction, indicating that you are putting no great emphasis on the error:

Your chairman's very understandable error reminds me of the lengthy letter which the mother and father of a boy at camp received from the camp leader. It said: "Robert is one of the best campers we have ever had." And it went on to tell about Robert's fine attitude, and how he was winning the admiration of his advisors and fellow-campers alike.

The mother answered the letter. She wrote: "Thank you for your very reassuring letter about Robert However, my boy is George—won't you tell me about *him?*"

NATIVE SON

(You are to introduce a returning home-town boy.)

Sometimes you have occasion to introduce a former resident of your community, who left it and is now returning, either to take up residence there again or for the purpose of addressing a meeting. It is always helpful to the speaker to have the audience reminded that he is a former resident, "a home-town boy," again "one of us." For that purpose, the following story is helpful:

In introducing John Blank to you this evening, I am reminded of the minister who, at the close of his sermon, asked all those who wanted to go to heaven to stand up. All but one man stood. The minister turned to him and said, "Don't you want to go to heaven?" "No," said the man. The minister said, "Where do you want to go?" And the man answered, "I don't want to go any place. I like it here!" That's what John Blank decided; after all, he likes it here.

And I take this opportunity to tell him that we like him here, too.

NEUTRALITY

(As chairman, you need to maintain neutrality between representatives of opposing political parties, of opposing factions, etc.)

If you are to preside at a meeting at which people of competing political parties are to debate, or representatives of opposing views will be stating their respective positions, it is almost always true that you will have the obligation of treating the speakers with complete impartiality. You should, of course, see to it that they have equal time, that there are no interruptions, and that you make it clear to the speakers and to the audience that you are not in any respect favoring either side. In this connection, you may wish to tell them the following:

Whatever my personal views may be on the matters that are to be discussed this evening, I shall do my best to indicate no preference whatever, and to stifle whatever tendency I may have to lean in one direction or the other. I was even tempted to follow the example set by an elderly gentleman who was in the kind of position I am in tonight, and who was trying, as I am, to maintain strict neutrality. He was to introduce two opposing candidates for sheriff. He said to the audience, "Now I want to present the first of the two men who will be speaking to us this evening. I have read his campaign literature and I can tell you that he is a remarkably intelligent, thoroughly industrious, impeccably honest, widely experienced, fully capable person, and that he most certainly deserves your vote for sheriff, in preference to his opponent, the second speaker. I now take pleasure in presenting . . ." and then he turned to the two candidates who were seated behind him and said, "Which of you two blokes wants to speak first?"

It sometimes happens that you are introducing a speaker whose views are not shared by the organization that he is addressing. This occurs, for example, when a Forum Society or a group of Government workers, obligated not to endorse a political candidate, nevertheless make their platform available to political candidates, one at a time, in a series. They do so for the purpose of hearing several candidates' views without endorsing any candidate. On such an occasion, after giving a resume of the speaker's background, it is well to remind the audience that the organization does not—and therefore you, as chairman of the meeting, cannot—either support or oppose the candidacy of the speaker. The following words have, on such occasions, proved highly acceptable to the audience:

As we are all aware, this organization makes its platform available to candidates, but it does not publicly endorse anyone. I am sure you all realize, therefore, that I have to content myself with a recitation of the speaker's educational and political background and stop there. Accordingly, without any words of commendation—and certainly without any words of condemnation—and without any indication as to whether he deserves either, I take pleasure in presenting Mr. George Jenkins.

After explaining that although the audience need not maintain a neutral attitude toward the speakers, you, as chairman, intend to do so very strictly, you may wish to use the following:

A group of people, with Mark Twain present, were discussing whether there was life after death, and the possibility of punishment after death. Following a rather lengthy conversation on the subject, during which Mark Twain maintained a strict silence, someone turned to him and said, "Mr. Clemens, what are your views—do you believe in heaven and hell?" The answer was: "You must excuse me; I have to be very careful what I say on that subject. I know I have friends in both places."

Pat Flaherty had been told by his doctor that he was on his deathbed, and he asked that a priest be called. The priest knew Pat well, and among other things knew that he was an old reprobate, so he said to him: "You have been told your condition is serious. Now, Pat, are you not ready, at last, to embrace the church and renounce the devil?" Pat thought about that for a moment and then replied, "Sure and I'm very ready to embrace the church, but Father, that part about renouncing the devil—do you think that in my situation I ought to take the risk of antagonizing *anybody?*"

As your chairman this evening, I shall keep that story in mind, because I intend to be strictly neutral—perhaps embracing both speakers but certainly not antagonizing either one.

I hope you all realize what a difficult job I have tonight. No matter what my views are on the subject to be discussed, and no matter how convincing or unconvincing I find either of the two speakers, I have the obligation of remaining completely neutral. I promise therefore that no matter what my views are now or will be during the course of the evening, I shall not betray them to you. I am reminded of the very sweet young lady who found herself at a dinner meeting seated between a rabbi and a bishop. Said she to her two dinner partners, "I feel as if I were a leaf between the Old Testament and the New Testament." And the bishop replied, "You will be sorry to hear, madam, that that page is always blank."

As your blank page, let me now introduce the first of the two speakers.

As your chairman this evening, I intend to maintain a quiet neutrality. After all, a moderator should be one who moderates his own reactions and in a strictly unbiased way permits the debaters to do the debating.

I am going to be like that very minor official at the bullfights—I am merely going to open and close the door to let the bull in and out.

NEWCOMER

(You are introducing a speaker who is new to the audience.)

Although it is almost always true that the speaker you are introducing has not previously appeared before this audience, you might, on some occasions, wish to mention that fact in a way which will be of some reassurance to the speaker. Thus, you might say, after reviewing background facts about him:

When Harry S. Truman was first elected to the U.S. Senate, Senator J. Ham. Lewis, a senator from Illinois, shook hands with Truman and welcomed him to the Senate. And then Senator Lewis said to the newly inducted Senator Truman, "Harry, don't be hesitant about speaking. It's true that for the first few months you'll be wondering how you ever got here. But after that, you'll be wondering how the rest of us ever got here."

Mr. _____, I know this is your first speech to our group, and I just want to say that during the course of it, you may wonder how you got here, but when you hear from us in the question period, you'll probably be wondering how we got here.

NOISE

(There is a sudden noise outside the hall.)

Sometimes a speaker has to suffer through noises outside the hall—trays being dropped, dishes being broken, loud talking by people who do not know that a meeting is in progress, etc. The audience is usually as troubled as the speaker, and the latter can often relieve the situation by referring to the noises rather than trying to ignore them. For example:

I think I can explain that interruption. Some time ago I saw an advertisement in *Variety* which, as you know, is the leading periodical for the acting profession. There are always numerous "situation wanted" ads in *Variety* and one of those, not too long ago, read: "Available for acting part—any part. Would accept job as dead body or for noises offstage." Apparently that fellow got his job right here.

NUMEROUS SPEAKERS

(You are to introduce several speakers.)

When there are several speakers on the program the chairman has to keep things moving along. Almost always speakers take longer than the time assigned to them—longer than they themselves estimate in advance. If the chairman does not exercise influence in the direction of shorter speeches the audience often becomes restive, some of them leave earlier than they otherwise would or find fault with the fact that the meeting was drawn out, and the general reaction militates against good attendance at the next meeting.

There are several ways in which a chairman can guard against these bad reactions. The most obvious way, of course, is to talk privately to each of the speakers in advance, telling him how many minutes have been allotted to him. This should be done, if possible, when the various speakers are first contacted but, more importantly, each speaker should be reminded individually at the meeting before the speaking begins.

A most effective way of keeping speeches brief is to inform the audience when the chairman is making his opening remarks that because there are several speakers each has had his speaking time very much restricted. This is as far as a chairman can properly go if the speakers have been allotted different lengths of time. But if the speakers have each been given the same length of time, the time should actually be announced. If the audience knows that each of the speakers has fifteen minutes in which to make his talk, it is a bold speaker indeed who will exceed the announced time limit. And if he does, the chairman can without embarrassment rap his gavel or even rise from his seat to indicate his readiness to introduce the next speaker, and any action can be counted upon to have prompt effect. Even if the chairman makes no move when the time limit has expired, audience reaction will almost always get the "message" to the speaker that he should be ending his remarks.

When a speaker has launched on his speech and gives evidence of ignoring the time limitation, it is not inappropriate for the chairman to deliver a little reminder to him. This should, of course, be done as unobtrusively as possible. It should therefore be done by means of a little note, not handed to the speaker but laid upon the rostrum. And if the chairman is seated next to the speaker while the latter is on his feet the note can be—and certainly should be—delivered without the chairman's rising from his chair.

The wording of the note is important, because every attempt should be made not to antagonize the speaker. It should be couched in gentle language and yet should deliver the message. Such a note might be worded in one of the following ways:

"Sorry—you have only two minutes more."

. . . . .

"Time is up in two minutes. (Wish we could have more.)"

. . . . .

"Regretful reminder: two more minutes."

Even a note to the speaker, placed unobtrusively on the rostrum, is sometimes ignored by an eager speaker. There is, however, a device for limiting the length of speeches that is not only sure fire but that also creates a certain amount of hilarity. Before introducing the first speaker, the chairman announces that each of the speakers has been limited to, let us say, ten minutes; that he realizes that sometimes speakers inadvertently talk beyond the designated time limit; that he has resolved that this is not going to happen on this occasion, and to make sure it does not happen he has brought an alarm clock (which he displays).

Thereafter, as each speaker begins to talk, the chairman unobtrusively sets the alarm for the proper period. (The alarm clock must be tested beforehand because some cannot be reliably set for short periods. There are, however, timers, often used by cooks, which can be set for as little as two or three minutes.) You may depend upon it that when the alarm goes off, not only will the speaker bring his talk to a quick close but in addition the audience will find the chairman's method highly humorous. This method of enforcing the time limitation has the added advantage of somehow removing from the chairman any blame for interrupting the speaker. In fact, on the rare occasions when a speaker may evidence some displeasure at the loud interruption, if the chairman will simply shrug his shoulders and point to the alarm clock to indicate that he is powerless in the face of this inexorable sentinel, he will find that the audience is overwhelmingly on his side rather than on the speaker's.

◆–◆–◆–◆

A most effective and yet good-humored way of influencing speakers toward brevity is for the chairman to introduce the session with an appropriate anecdote, such as one of the following:

As you know, we are to hear from four speakers this evening. This means, of course, that each of them feels a great obligation to be brief. Let me remind them of the Spartans, who were well known for, among other things, their dislike of lengthy speeches.

It is told that a neighboring island was stricken with famine and the people on that island sent an envoy to Sparta to ask for food. He made a long, long plea, and at the end of it the spokesman for the Spartans said, "We don't remember any more what you said at the beginning. The end is confusing." And they sent him back without anything.

A second envoy was sent with empty bags and all he said was, "They are empty. Please fill them."

And they did. But when they had finished they said to this second envoy, "Next time remember that we can see that your bags are empty. You needn't have said so. Next time don't talk so long."

I just want to give our various speakers one message: I trust they will all remember that sometimes a speech is like a wheel—the longer the spoke the greater the tire.

Since there are several speakers on our program I ask each of them to consider the advice of a professional lecturer of my acquaintance on how to make a speech. He says that the thing to do is to think up a good beginning, and then think up a good ending, and then keep them as close together as possible.

I hope our speakers will keep in mind what happened one day when Henry Clay was a member of Congress. Clay and a fellow member were engaged in debate. At the end of a long boresome speech the other man turned to Clay and said, "The difference between us is that you, sir, speak only for the moment, and I speak for posterity." And Clay answered immediately, "And you seem determined to speak until your audience is here." And then he added, "By the way, don't you mean that I speak *by* the moment and you speak by the hour?"

I just want to remind the speakers that if their speeches are not kept short they run a risk that might not occur to them. On one occasion I attended a dinner at which I overheard one waiter say to another: "We'll get home early tonight. I waited on the head table, and when I took off the main course I picked up four pages of the speech."

I know each of our speakers will realize that there are other speakers with whom he is sharing the time. Perhaps I ought to remind them that when Pope John began his pontificate he was asked whether he planned to make as many addresses to the public as his predecessors had made. His answer was, "I hope to talk much less—but I hope to say as much."

I am sure our speakers will say a great deal even if they talk a very short time.

In view of the fact that we have several speakers on our program this evening I should like to tell them a little story—though I am perfectly willing to have the audience listen in. I have a good friend who doesn't care much for concerts. His wife loves them and often goads him into going with her. Recently when they were seated in the auditorium, a few minutes before the concert started she found her husband studying the program intently and even making notes in the margin opposite each of the musical selections listed. She was, of course, very pleased at this new interest on his part. She even said to herself that perhaps she had finally aroused his interest in symphonic music. Finally, her husband turned to her and said, "I've got it doped out; if everything goes well, we'll be out of here by 10:20."

I am sure that our speakers will cooperate, and you'll be out of here well before 10:20.

Each of our speakers is aware that he must leave time for his colleagues. Besides, I am sure that all of them learned long ago that if you don't strike oil in fifteen minutes you should stop boring.

Since we have a very full program with several speakers I must ask them to keep in mind Mark Twain's experience. One Sunday, with Mark Twain in the congregation, the minister made a special plea for a donation for the church's building fund, and as the collection plate was being passed, Twain listened to the plans for the new building as they were being outlined by the minister. He resolved to put $20 in the plate when it came to him. But as the minister droned on, he mentally reduced his donation to $10. A few minutes later when boredom was beginning to set in he decided to give only $5. But he confessed later that with the minister still talking when the collection plate reached him, he took $2 out.

I know that each of the persons on this program fully realizes that he is by no means the sole speaker, and that each of them, therefore, will do his job and quit, and leave as much time as he reasonably can for his collegues on the program, in the sound belief, of course, that they will do the same for him.

It might not be amiss, however, just to remind them of a little rhyme I ran across long ago:

> Whatever the topic he speaks on
> Be it earthly or even lunar
> He has a fine grasp of his subject
> But he ought to let go of it sooner.

Since we have several speakers this evening, I take this opportunity to remind them publicly of their obligation to keep their speeches short. I might even be able to scare them into even briefer speeches by telling them about Jock MacPherson. Poor Jock had been tried and found guilty of murder, and was sentenced to be hanged. Having tried in every way, unsuccessfully, to have his sentence set aside, he finally realized that his hanging was to take place the very next day. As a last resort, he asked the warden for pen and paper so that he could write a telegram to the Governor appealing to him to commute his sentence. The following morning when they came to take Jock MacPherson away to the gallows, his cell was strewn with paper and he had not sent any telegram. They discovered that he had not been able to get his telegram cut down to fifteen words for the minimum rate.

Now the moral I trust our speakers will get from this story is that if you don't keep your message short, your sentence can be death.

Thus far, our speakers have been mindful that there are other speakers and that the hands on the clock keep moving. Perhaps this is a good time to remind those from whom we are still to hear of the need for keeping their remarks within reasonable time limits. There is, in fact, a very appropriate little verse which I now read to them:

> Speakers who hope to see their words
> Enshrined at the heavenly portal
> Should remember a speech need never be
> Eternal, to be immortal.

I am sure they are all aware that the key to immortality as a speaker is brevity.

As you know, our program this evening includes several speakers. But please do not assume from that fact that this will be a long, late meeting. I assure you it will not, because I recall what Victor Borge once said about his piano.

He was telling a guest what a remarkable instrument his piano was. He was telling him about the tone, the pedals, the keys, and then he added: "And in addition to all that I can tell time by this piano." Naturally his guest registered his disbelief about that last point and so Victor Borge said: "I will show you," and he then sat down and played a few bars. Whereupon a man in the next apartment opened a window and shouted: "You idiot—stop that playing! Don't you know it is 1:30 in the morning!"

I am assuring you that this meeting will not be unduly lengthy because I am not going to risk the possibility that any of you will be shouting: "You idiot—don't you know it is 11:00 at night!"

Since there are several speakers on the program this evening, I know that each of them will keep in mind that he must sacrifice a few minutes of his own speech in order to make sure that all the speakers will have equal opportunity. This is an "equal opportunity" organization!

I am therefore asking that each of them remember this little verse:

> His command of the language
> Has only one fault:
> How rarely he gives it
> A command to halt.

I feel sure that each of the speakers will make sure that this little ditty is inappropriate in his case.

Still another way of reminding speakers that there are several on the program and that therefore each should try to leave time for the others, is to say:

I trust that each of the speakers will remember that there are fellow speakers on the program and that we shall have a question period at the end of the speaking, and we want to leave time for that too.

Perhaps we should remind them that we ought to take as a warning the sign outside a Chicago barber shop which read:

"Six Barbers. Continuous Discussion!"

In our case we need time for each speaker's individual contribution and for audience participation.

Finally, there is another device a chairman can use to keep the program moving along smoothly—a whistle. Like an alarm clock, a whistle is effective and has a humorous aspect for the audience. You would announce in advance that there are several speakers and that you are therefore going to be very cruel in keeping them within strict time limits, for the benefit of both the audience and the other speakers, and that the instrument you are using for that purpose is a whistle. At that point, a sample blast on the whistle will amuse speakers and audience alike. You then add that the whistle brings up a story:

An American manufacturer was acting as host at his factory to a visiting Russian, a production chief from Moscow. They were on a tour of the plant when, exactly at twelve noon, the factory whistle blew even louder than the one the audience just heard.

At once the workers streamed out of the plant. In great excitement, the Russian shouted to his host, "They're escaping! Do something to keep them in the factory!"

The American manufacturer tried to reassure him. "Don't worry," he said, "they'll be back."

At one o'clock, the whistle blew again. To the Russian's surprise, all the workers streamed back into the factory. "Now," said the American, "let's talk about your order for those machines."

Said the Russian, "Never mind the machines. How much do you want for that whistle?"

You can end this anecdote by stating:

Somehow I doubt that my whistle will please the speakers as much as that other whistle pleased the Russian—but I trust it will be just as effective.

OLD AGE

(You are to introduce an elderly person.)

Although the uninitiated might think that introducing an elderly person by reference to his age would be resented, long platform experience indicates that quite the reverse is true. The fact is that a person who reaches his 90's or even his 80's and is still alert and active is usually very proud of the fact. He enjoys having his friends allude to his age, and one who introduces him should feel completely safe in doing so. The following would be appropriate:

Mr. _____ has a great advantage over most of us. He has had many more years of experience. He has learned much more than you and I. He is more expert in various ways. I envy him very much.

In fact, I had a conversation with my doctor not long ago on this subject. He said to me, "You must understand that I can't make you young again." And I said to him, "I don't want to be young again. In fact, I have an entirely different ambition—I just want to keep on getting older."

◆ ◆ ◆ ◆

I am always glad to introduce a person who is more experienced and wiser than most of us. To qualify in those respects, you have to be a little older than most of us. Perhaps the reason why Mr. _____ is not at all backward about stating his age is that he knows very well that he is not just older than most of us but also more experienced and wiser.

In any case, whatever the reason, he is altogether unlike the lady I read about not long ago who visited Las Vegas. She had never seen a roulette table before, but had resolved to gamble. With a large stack of chips in her hand, she watched people as they played roulette, and finally she said, "I want to play roulette, but this is my first time, and I don't understand the game. How do I pick the number to bet on?" Someone spoke up immediately, saying, "Play your age." The lady thought a moment and finally put a whole stack of chips—representing a large amount of money—on number 35. The ball rolled around and finally landed on 42—and the lady fainted.

Mr. _____ will never lose money that way.

If it is a lively oldster whom you are to introduce, you may ıt to use the following:

I think our speaker, Mr. Blank, considers himself rather elderly—but I know him and I don't. When I see him in action, I am reminded of the three old men who were discussing the best way, in their respective opinions, of leaving this life. The first one said that he would like to go quickly—get hit by a speeding car. The second one said he would like to go still faster and surer—in a jet-propelled plane. But the third man said, "Well, I've often thought about it and I have decided I'd rather go another way. I want to be shot by a jealous husband."

I'm not sure, but I think Mr. Blank could have been that third man.

In introducing our speaker, I want to make clear that I realize that old age is a relative thing. Our speaker may be old in years, but not in any other way.

In fact, he reminds me of a coed who brought home from college, one vacation, a very attractive young blonde and introduced her to her grandfather. Then she turned to her young classmate and said, "I just want you to know that grandad is in his nineties."

Whereupon grandad said with a smile to the visitor, "And I just want you to know that I'm in my *early* nineties."

And I can imagine our speaker saying that—but many, many years from now, of course.

PHYSICAL INJURY

(You wear a bandage or other evidence of recent physical injury.)

If it should become necessary for you to address an audience at a time when there is some visible evidence of your having suffered an injury, it is best to say a word about it. A bandage or other such badge of impairment is bound to attract attention and will, in fact, distract the audience if unexplained. The better course is to tell the audience what happened to you as briefly as you can, underplaying the extent of the injury. And you might then add:

> I am reminded of the small boy who had to be vaccinated. And when the job was completed and the boy had put on his coat, ready to leave, the doctor said, "Let me put a bandage around your arm, over your coat sleeve, so that people will be careful not to run into you or jostle you." The boy said, "That's fine," and held out his right arm for that purpose. The doctor laughed and said, "That's not the arm that's vaccinated, it's the other one." The boy answered, "I know that—but you don't know our neighborhood."

PROMINENT PERSON

(The speaker is very well known.)

For introducing a very well-known person, here's a bit of advice: don't tell your audience that the speaker "needs no introduction." Not only is that one of the oldest cliches uttered from a platform, but it is untrue; every speaker has to be introduced. Even the President of the United States is introduced—with the same six words each time.

A person of prominence is almost always active in many circles—business, club, charitable, social, etc. In such cases, consider the following:

> Our speaker this evening calls to my mind a little story about the company that sent a collection item to a small town, addressed to the postmaster. The letter asked the postmaster to recommend a lawyer who could be hired to collect an account from someone living in that town.
>
> They received in reply a letter which said, "I am the postmaster and I have received your letter. I am also a lawyer, but I would not take a case from an outsider against one of our local citizens. Besides, I am that citizen who you say owes you the money. I would like, in conclusion, to tell you where to go—but I happen also to be the pastor of our Baptist Church."
>
> Our speaker fills many more roles than that.

Then describe his various connections.

PTA MEETINGS

(You are addressing mothers or fathers, or both.)

A story that indicates some connection with—or at least an understanding of—the problems facing an audience helps to produce rapport. The following are of use when you are speaking to parents (but only if their children are not present!):

> I want to assure you at the outset that I do have some inkling of the frustrations and difficulties of parents. In

fact, I would like to say a word on behalf of mothers, by way of a very short story:

I happened to walk into a neighbor's house not long ago, when a mother was entertaining her little boy. As I came into the room, the little boy was shouting "Bang! Bang!" and the mother was slumping to the floor. But when she did not rise after a moment or two, I went over to her and said, "Can I help you?" Her answer was, "Quiet! This is the only chance I get for a rest!"

Or you may prefer the following, after suggesting that you are indeed aware of some of the problems connected with the rearing of adolescents:

One of the questions often included in an application for life insurance is: "Have you ever been declared feebleminded, retarded or insane?" I've always resented that question. I think they ought to add—"That is, except by your own children."

QUESTION PERIOD

(Drawing questions from the audience; "fielding" the questions, etc.)

It often happens—more frequently these days than in the past—that an audience is told either in the written announcement of a speech or at the meeting that when the speaker has finished, the audience will be invited to ask questions. But the questions are not always readily forthcoming, and this creates a special problem. In order to prevent what might otherwise be a somewhat embarrassing silence, it is best to interrupt it by saying something like this:

Somebody has said that getting questions out of an audience is a little like getting olives out of a jar. It's always hard to get the first one. After that they come pouring out. Well, who has the first one?

And if that doesn't work, you might try the following:

Please understand that you can ask questions free of charge! I began to think that perhaps you were not asking questions because you remembered the young man who went to a gypsy fortuneteller, and when she had finished reading his palm and telling him about the future she said,

"Now you are entitled to ask two questions for ten dollars." And the young man said, "Ten dollars! Isn't that awfully high for just two questions?" And the gypsy replied, "Yes, it is. Now, what is your second question?"

And you might wish to add:

Of course, here, you only get one question each—but it's free. Now—who has a question?

Other anecdotes that fit the question-period situation are the following:

Perhaps you remember the story of the speaker who at the close of his address asked the audience if they had any questions. Immediately a young man stood up at the rear of the hall and asked a question. The speaker answered it in some detail and so extremely well that the audience applauded when he finished. The speaker then asked if there were other questions, and after a moment the same young man stood up and said, "Since no one else is asking any questions perhaps I could ask another one"—and he proceeded to do so. Again the speaker answered so well that the audience once more broke into hearty applause. After a moment's silence, the same young man stood up once more, but this time he said to the speaker, "I just can't remember—what was that third question you told me to ask you?"

I am sure we were all very glad to have Mr. Blank as our speaker this evening. We arranged in advance that he was to put a little icing on the cake by agreeing to answer questions at the close of his speech. As we go into the question period, I recall the conversation that took place between a little old lady and an elevator operator. As the elevator ascended, she said to him, "Don't you ever feel sick going up and down this way?" "Yes," he said. "Is it the motion going up?" she asked. "No," he said. "Is it the sudden stops?" "No," he said. "Then, what is it that makes you sick?" "It's the questions," he said.

However, our speaker assures me that he doesn't feel that way about questions at all. So, who has the first one?

We have now reached a question period and I want to encourage you to enter into it. I hope you will remember the story about the little boy walking along with his father and asking him questions. He said, "Dad, what makes the thunder?" And the father answered, "Son, I really can't answer that question." A little farther along, the boy said, "Dad, last night I saw a falling star. What makes that?" His father answered, "I'm sorry, son. I really don't know."

A few minutes later the boy said, "I always wonder when I see an airplane, how such a heavy thing can stay up in the air. How does that work?" And his father answered, "I wish I knew, but I really can't explain that."

Whereupon the boy said, "Dad, I'm not bothering you with these questions, am I?" And his father answered, "Of course not, son. How else are you going to learn about things unless you ask questions."

And so I say to you: How are you going to learn about things unless you ask questions? I think I'd better add that I thoroughly believe you will have better luck tonight obtaining answers than the boy I was telling you about.

It is sometimes difficult to start questioning from the audience after the speaker has concluded his main address. In that connection, the following should prove helpful:

> Let me encourage you to question our speaker. Sometimes questions develop highly interesting answers. For example, an army colonel was addressing an audience of army recruits who had been very recently drafted. When the colonel finished his talk, he asked if there were any questions. There was silence for a while and then he heard one of the recruits saying to another, "Go ahead. Ask him! Don't be scared."
>
> The audience laughed but the colonel said very seriously, "That's right. Ask whatever you have in mind— no matter what."
>
> Finally a young draftee said, "Colonel, don't you think there are too many colonels in the army?"
>
> The colonel thought a moment and when the laughter subsided, he answered, "Yes, I think there are. What this army needs is one less colonel and one more general."

Sometimes a very difficult and abstruse question is asked, and one feels the need of easing the situation and perhaps gaining an extra minute or two for thinking before answering. In that situation, the following will prove helpful:

> I'm always hoping for easy questions, but as you see, things don't work that way. Of course, some speakers have the ability to think up an easy answer even when the question is difficult. For instance, I heard about a speaker who was faced with the question: "Can you tell me the total United States export of coal for any given year? The speaker thought a moment and then said, "Certainly. 1492—none."

◆━◆━◆━◆

You may find that occasionally, in response to the suggestion that questions are in order, a listener will make an impudent remark in the guise of a question. For example, such a person might say, "I have a question. Where did you ever get the idea that we would fall for what you are telling us?"—or he may put some other insulting statement to you in the form of a query.

On such occasions, it is very tempting to respond with an equally insulting remark, but that kind of reply not only gives satisfaction to the questioner—because he has succeeded in angering you—but also runs the risk of antagonizing others in the audience. The more experienced a speaker is, the more convinced he becomes that a cool answer is far better than a hot one.

No matter what the statement happens to be, if it is in the form of a question, there is at least one response that fits all such inquiries: "I will forgive you for asking that question if you will forgive me for not answering it. Now, who has the next question?"

You will find that most audiences will applaud that statement. Most audiences, with any encouragement from the speaker, will react against interruptions or insults from whatever source.

QUESTION POSERS

(Handling embarrassing questions.)

The chairman has invited questions and I hope I am able to answer them; and if not, I hope somebody will make convincing excuses for me. I have in mind the immigrant father who was watching his son on television. His son was answering questions when that "$64,000 Question" program was on. As each question was asked and his son produced each successful answer, the father, sitting in his living room, would say to the family, "That's my Tony." But finally, the son was asked the final question for the $64,000 jackpot: Who shot Abraham Lincoln? His mind went blank and he simply could not come up with the name and finally had to admit defeat. Whereupon his proud father stood up and shouted, "That's my Tony; he wouldn't squeal on anybody."

Now let's have the questions—but try to think up as good an alibi as that one if I should miss.

REHASH OF PREVIOUS SPEECH

(Previous speaker "steals" your main points.)

It sometimes happens when there are several speakers on the program that someone who speaks before you do makes the very point you had intended to present. In such situations, the following may be useful:

A funny thing happened to me tonight—not on the way to this meeting but after I arrived. Mr. Blank has "stolen" a large part of my speech. Of course he did it unwittingly and without knowing what I was going to say, and so no blame attaches to what he has done. In fact, I feel complimented that his thinking ran in the same direction as mine. I recall that when a similar thing occurred to Adlai Stevenson he said to the audience when his turn came: "Ladies and gentlemen, I was very pleased to see how enthusiastically you received Mr. X's speech. At first I was surprised to hear Mr. X saying what I was prepared to say this evening, but I soon realized what had happened— Mr. X picked up my speech and left me his. I assure you that his speech, which I have before me, is not nearly as good as mine, and I'm not going to give it. Instead, let me just emphasize some of the things in that beautiful address of mine which you have already heard."

Ladies and gentlemen, that is all I can do too—but at least I have a fine precedent for handling the situation this way.

◆—◆—◆—◆

Or perhaps you would prefer the following:

I must report to you that a very peculiar coincidence has occurred. What I had prepared to say this evening has already been said, in essence, by Mr. Blank. Of course you are the beneficiaries of that coincidence, because I shall speak not nearly as long as I had intended. It may seem long—but it won't be. It puts me in mind of a much less felicitous coincidence which ran like this:

A dinner was being given to celebrate the 25th anniversary of the ordination of a priest. When he was called upon to speak, he told of his early discouragement when he had first taken up his duties. He told of the fact that the first person who came to confess to him recounted a whole series of sinful and criminal acts for which he was asking absolution. "I began to wonder," he said, "whether the whole community was that way. But, as time went on, I was very pleased to find that that incident was never duplicated by anyone else of all the thousands of people who have confessed to me in these 25 years." He then went on to tell of the satisfactions and joys he had experienced during that quarter century of service.

Shortly after he had finished, the audience broke into applause as the governor of the state entered the hall, made his way to the rostrum, and shook hands with the priest. And turning to the microphone, the governor said: "I'm sorry I was delayed. I wanted to be here to be among the first to congratulate this wonderful man, because I was the first person who ever confessed to him when he became a priest."

I am sure you will agree that tonight's coincidence is a much happier one.

REPEATER

(The speaker has addressed the audience on previous occasions.)

When the speaker has addressed the same group on a previous occasion, it is well to mention the fact. The fact that he has been invited to talk to this audience more than once is not only complimentary to the speaker, but also puts the audience in a more receptive mood. The following story serves both purposes:

We are glad to welcome Mr. _____. He is no stranger to this audience, having spoken at our invitation on a prior occasion. His presence here reminds me of the fact that some years ago England's famous Black Watch Regiment was sent on a world tour. They appeared on the streets of New York for a marching exhibition. Their leader was interviewed on television and he was asked whether the Black Watch Regiment had ever appeared here before. "Yes," he answered, "in 1776."

Mr. _____ has appeared here before, but much more recently than that. And there's another difference: his prior appearance was a victory—and that's why he was invited here again tonight.

◆━◆━◆━◆━◆

Our guest speaker this evening, as you are aware, has spoken to us on a previous occasion.

Perhaps you know about the man who was applying for a job and his prospective employer asked him whether he had any letter of recommendation from his previous employer. The man said, "Yes, I do, and here it is," and he handed over a short letter that said: "To Whom It May Concern—John Henderson worked for us for one week and we were satisfied."

Our guest this evening on a previous occasion spoke to us for one hour and we were satisfied. But in our case, we were so thoroughly satisfied that we invited him to return, and here he is.

If you are a speaker who has addressed the same organization on a previous occasion, the chairman may very well include that fact in introducing you. In that case, you may want to begin your presentation with one of the following:

Your chairman is correct in saying that I have had the privilege of addressing this organization on a prior occasion. I want to start, therefore, by assuring you that I do not intend to make the same speech I made then. I have in mind an incident involving a speaker who had addressed the same audience ten years before his current appearance and the chairman, in introducing him, told the audience that the speaker would be addressing them on the subject of "Adventuring Through the Universe."

The chairman then went on to say that the same speaker had addressed the organization ten years earlier, and while leafing through some notes the chairman added, "I think I have a memo here of the speaker's subject on that earlier occasion. Yes, here it is—his subject ten years ago was—oh, my! 'Adventuring Through the Universe.' "

When the speaker, somewhat red faced, came to the podium, he said "Ladies and gentlemen, I am afraid it is true. It's the same old speech. But you have to remember— it's the same old universe!"

In my case, things are a little different. I may, of course, give you the same old speech—but at least I had sense enough not to give it the same old title.

You may remember the alumnus who returned to his college and called on one of his professors who, at the time, was in the process of giving his students an examination. The visiting alumnus was astonished upon reading the questions in the examination to find that they were very familiar. And he said to the professor, "It seems to me that this examination is identical with the one you gave my class when I was in college years ago!"

Said the professor, "Of course it is. But you have to remember that although the questions are the same today, the answers are entirely different."

Here are some other approaches you can use in this situa- on:

As you know, I was invited to speak to your organization on a previous occasion. Your Program Committee took a big chance in inviting me for a second time. For all they know I may have only one speech to give, in which case this would be mere repetition.

You may remember when the *Saturday Evening Post* was alive, about three or four times a year it featured a story by Clarence Buddington Kelland. On one occasion when Kelland was in the office of the *Saturday Evening*

Post he said to the editor, "I'll have my new story ready for you in a couple of weeks," and the editor answered, "That's fine. But remember—don't go changing that plot."

I learned from that little tale that you can dress up a story in many different ways so that is isn't recognizable as the same story. I assure you that the talk I am about to give isn't the same as I gave last time I had the pleasure of addressing you—or if it is, you'll never recognize it.

◆——◆——◆——◆

As your chairman has said, I have spoken to this organization on previous occasions and there must be some people in this audience who have heard me before. I feel the obligation, therefore, not to give you any mere repetition in another form of what I have told this audience previously. I must not, under any circumstances, let myself get in the position in which Sir Alec Guinness, the British star, found himself when he was a naval captain in World War II. He was on convoy duty and, for some reason, he found it almost impossible to keep his ship in line with the other ships in the convoy, and he was repeatedly getting blinker messages which read "Hebrew 13-8." At first Guinness's crew thought it was a rugby score, but he assured them that it was a reference to the Bible. When a Bible was finally produced Hebrew 13-8 read: "Jesus Christ, the same yesterday, and today, and forever."

I give you my solemn vow that my topic today and my treatment of it are not going to justify any such almost sacrilegious biblical reference.

REPORT

(You are making a report—results of a survey, annual report, progress report, etc.)

Reports are often dull affairs. To the extent that they can be lightened by appropriate anecdotes, the better your chance of getting the attention of the audience and holding it. For that purpose:

In connection with this report, I must tell you about the announcement which a pilot made to the passengers on board his plane. A few hours after take-off, the pilot turned on his intercom and said: "Ladies and gentlemen, I have two announcements to make; one is bad, the other is very good. Let me give you the bad one first: we are absolutely lost. Our compass and all other equipment having to do with location have gone out of order. Neither the navigator nor I has the slightest idea where we are heading. We may be going in any of the four directions; we cannot tell. But now let me give you the good news: we have a 200-mile-an-hour tail wind and we're making wonderful time!"

I tell you about that plane because our organization is so different. We know exactly where we are headed; we are working steadfastly toward our goals and our direction does not vary. I often think—and no doubt some of you do too—that we aren't going as fast as we should go. But you have to remember that we have no outside force helping us; we furnish the only tail wind we have. With your help, we shall certainly get there—and in good time.

SMALL AUDIENCE

(The audience is distressingly small.)

Sometimes far fewer people show up than were expected. If you are the speaker on such an occasion you might like to begin with one of the following:

I notice that the room is not filled to overflowing. Some of you might even have wondered whether I would be willing to speak to a small audience—but let me reassure you on that point by telling you about the speaker who, when he arrived at the hall ready to take the platform, found that there was only one person present. He waited for others to arrive but no one else came. So he went to the one-man audience and said to him: "I came here to make a speech, as you know. Do you think I ought to go ahead with it?" And the man answered: "Well, I'm from Montana and all I know is cattle. And I know that if I took a load of feed down to the cattle and only one steer showed up, I certainly would feed him."

Accordingly, the speaker took the platform and began his talk. Despite the size of his audience, as he talked he began to get warmed up, and soon he was raising his voice, pounding the rostrum, shaking his fist and emphasizing every sentence with wild gestures as if he were talking to a thousand people.

An hour later when he finished, he came off the platform and said to his one-man audience: "Well, what did you think of my speech?" And the man answered: "Well, you know, I come from Montana, and all I know is cattle;

if I took a load of feed down to the cattle and only one steer showed up, I sure wouldn't give him the whole load."

But I'm different, ladies and gentlemen—I'm happy to give you the whole load.

I notice that there are not too many people here this evening. It puts me in mind of the small boy who said to his father: "I'm supposed to tell you that there's going to be a small PTA meeting tomorrow night." And his father said, "Well, if it's going to be a small one, do I have to go?" And the boy answered, "Oh yes. It's just you and me and the principal."

I suppose you would consider this audience a small one, but I have heard of still smaller audiences. I remember the minister who announced one Sunday morning, "We will have our regular prayer meeting Wednesday night. Perhaps some of you will decide to attend. You will find the janitor and me praying together as usual."

I realize that fewer people turned out this evening than were expected. I remember a story that Abraham Lincoln often told on himself. He made a speech to a very small audience while a blizzard was raging outside. When he finished there was hardly any applause, and there were actually some hisses and boos. After the audience had filed out, the janitor helped Mr. Lincoln on with his coat and, noticing how depressed he was, said to him, "Mr. Lincoln, don't pay any attention to the way the audience treated you. They don't have any sense. Anybody with any sense stayed home tonight."

You had better respond well to my talk this evening or I'll be recalling that janitor's sympathetic comment about the audience.

SPEAKING WITHOUT FEE

(The speaker is to have no honorarium.)

Many speakers who would normally be given a fee in payment for the time and trouble involved in preparing a speech, attending the meeting, etc., are willing to appear and speak without charge when the organization is one in which they hold an office or whose purposes they deeply wish to further.

On such occasions, it is not amiss—and the speaker is often flattered by it—to remind the audience of the speaker's reputation and the fact that he is in demand as a speaker, but that he volunteered to speak to this audience without a fee because of his interest in its goals. In that connection, the following is useful:

I therefore want to thank Mr. Blank for being with us this evening and foregoing his usual honorarium. I must say, however, that I am reminded of a small boy who stood on the corner with just two or three newspapers under his arm, shouting the headlines at the top of his voice. The first man who stopped to buy a paper said to him, "I've never seen you on this corner before. Are you making any money?" The boy answered, "No, I'm not making any money. I pay ten cents for the paper and I sell it for ten cents." "Well," said the man, "why are you out here selling newspapers?" And the boy answered, "Because I don't care if I don't make any money—as long as I get a chance to holler."

I know that Mr. Blank is talking to us on one of his

favorite subjects, and although he is not making any money tonight, at least we are giving him a chance to holler.

◆ ◆ ◆ ◆ ◆

If instead of introducing a speaker who is not charging an honorarium, you yourself are the speaker donating his services, and if the chairman mentions this in his introduction, you may respond with the following:

It was generous of the chairman to compliment me as he did and to mention the fact that I am speaking without fee. I hope no one will rise to offer a motion along the lines of one I heard about some years ago. The chairman had announced, as your chairman did just now, that the speaker was not charging any fee, and he added that this would help the organization's treasury considerably. Whereupon one of the members of the organization rose and said, "Mr. Chairman, I move that the money be used to get better speakers in the future."

If you happen to feel that way when I finish, all I ask is that you withhold all motions until after I have left the meeting.

Another story in this connection, which is "adjustable" for either the speaker or introducer, is the following:

When the chairman of your program committee asked me if I would speak to you tonight, he also asked me what my fee would be. I told him that there were certain subjects in which I was greatly interested and that therefore, if he would let me select the subject of my talk this evening, my fee would be zero, but that if he selected the subject, my fee would be $100. But then I told him also that, either way, I would give the same speech. Of course, he then promptly told me that I could select the subject—and this explains why I am foregoing any honorarium tonight.

SUBSTITUTION

(You are substituted for a previously announced speaker.)

It occasionally happens that because of extremely bad weather, sudden illness or other emergency, a scheduled speaker finds himself forced to cancel the engagement—sometimes at the last hour. On such occasions, if you are to be substituted as the speaker, you should be aware that the audience is almost bound to be disappointed when you announce that the person they came to hear will not be speaking. A story like the following should ingratiate you:

Like you, I was disappointed that Mr. Blank is not going to be with us this evening; and, on hearing that I was to take his place, I venture to say that I was not any more delighted than you! I shall, of course, do my best to fill his shoes—although that, as I am sure you will agree, is not easy for anybody to do.

The situation reminds me of the time when a famous baseball player by the name of Pat O'Malley had become the hero of his home town. His enthusiastic followers had decided to present him with an automobile, and just prior to the opening of the ball game on a given day, a beautiful Cadillac was presented to Pat.

The ball game followed, and in the 8th inning with the score tied, Pat's team had three men on the bases with two out and it was Pat's turn to bat. Now he had made his name as a fielder, not as a batter, and the manager decided that on this occasion, despite the celebration for Pat, he would send up a pinch-hitter. So, after a few moments of delay, the announcement came over the loudspeaker: "Miguel Salvador now batting for O'Malley!" Immediately, up stood a big giant of a fellow in the grandstand, and in stentorian tones he announced: "Flanagan now leaving the ballpark!"

With that story in the back of my mind, I was, of course, relieved to see that all of you seem to have decided to stay in your seats, in spite of the announcement that I was to be a pinch-hitter. Of course, if my fee for this evening were a Cadillac, I might not care quite so much; but as it is, I very much appreciate your staying with me while I take my turn at bat.

If you are called upon to substitute for another speaker, previously announced, it is always well to play down your role and at the same time establish as good a rapport with the audience as possible from the outset. The following might help:

> If you are disappointed at the fact that the scheduled speaker is unable to be here, and that I have been substituted, I can understand your disappointment. However, I hope you will take it the way an expectant father, pacing the halls of the hospital, took the news about his first-born. When a nurse told him that the baby had arrived, she said to him, "What did you want—a girl or a boy?" He promptly answered, "A boy." The nurse said, "Well, you have a girl." And the father promptly answered, "Oh, well, that's not too bad. After all, a girl was my second choice."
>
> I just hope you will be equally philosophical in accepting me. In fact, I am hoping I was your second choice.

The following story is appropriate either when you are substituted for a speaker who has failed to appear or when you are introducing a substitute speaker. In the latter case, for example, you would first explain the reasons for the absence of the previously announced speaker and then you would add the following:

Fortunately, we have been able to bring you an excellent speaker to take his place. Before I introduce him, let me tell you a little story:

Some years ago the famous Henry Ward Beecher was scheduled to speak one Sunday morning as the guest pastor in a New York church and, as you would expect, the church was packed with people. But Henry Ward Beecher was taken ill. And his brother, who was also a minister, came to the church to take his well-known brother's place. As soon as the audience became aware of the substitution, some of them began to leave, but the president of the congregation took care of that. Said he, "All those who came here this morning to worship Henry Ward Beecher should feel free to leave. Those who came to worship God will stay, of course."

Tonight, as I said, our scheduled speaker is unable to be here. I assume all those in the audience who came to hear an excellent speech by an excellent speaker will stay. I am sure you will be glad you did.

TACTLESS REMARKS

(You have inadvertently made a tactless remark.)

It happens to almost all of us: we say something we wish we hadn't. When this occurs in the course of an address to an audience, it is, of course, doubly embarrassing. As soon as you realize the full import of what you have said, it is best to refer to it and, in order to relieve your own and the audience's tension, try an anecdote:

I have just uttered something that might have been better left unsaid. In my gross lack of tact, I remind myself of the fellow who, upon encountering a young woman he had not seen for a considerable time, said to her, "You have gotten quite a little stouter, haven't you?" She said, "Now, now, you know you shouldn't ever tell a woman she's getting fat." And he answered, "Oh, I'm sorry. I didn't think a woman your age would mind at all."

◆—◆—◆—◆—◆

I realize now that I said something a few moments ago that I should not have said. That's what happens when you don't follow the warning notice I saw hanging in the room in which a large corporation holds its board meetings. It said, "Be sure brain is working before putting mouth in gear."

◆—◆—◆—◆

I must interrupt myself and return to something I said a bit earlier. It was something which I now rather regret saying—and I think the best thing to do is to tell you so.

I feel very much like the hostess who sat at the head of a long dinner table at which some twenty of her guests were eating dinner, and she wrote a little note, folded it several times, and sent it down to a woman at the far end of the table. When the note reached the woman, she handed it to the man on her left and said, "I don't have my glasses with me. Would you mind reading this note to me?" He then read aloud: "Don't neglect the man on your left. I know he's an awful bore, but talk to him anyhow"

TITLE MISTAKEN

(You are introduced by the wrong title.)

I find I have to correct your chairman in one respect [You then make the correction.]

This slight error reminds me of the employee who, upon receiving his paycheck, promptly went to his boss and said, "My check is wrong. You have underpaid me by $1.00." His boss answered, "Last week you were overpaid $2.00, but we didn't hear a single word out of you." Said the employee: "Of course not. I wouldn't complain about one mistake, but two in succession—I can't keep silent about that."

So I suppose I should not have said a word about it. After all, it was only one mistake—and not a very serious one at that.

◆——◆——◆——◆

Your chairman, in his introduction, has referred to me as _____. I appreciate that reference, but it does not happen to apply to me and I thought I ought to correct it. Incidentally, it reminds me of the very kind and sympathetic lady who was being guided through the halls of an insane asylum. As she was very much interested in how the inmates were being treated she stopped the first man she came upon and asked him how long he had been there. He answered that he had been there about 12 years. She then asked him whether he was satisfied with the treatment he was getting and he said yes, he had no complaints at all. But then, with a smile, he said, "Perhaps you are not aware that I am the superintendent here." Said the lady: "Oh, I am very sorry. This will be a lesson to me. I'll never judge by appearances again."

TWO-SESSION MEETINGS

(The audience is to reassemble at another session.)

Conventions are often called for two-day or three-day sessions. If you are presiding at one of the earlier sessions, at its close you will want to remind those present that they are to meet again the following day at a certain time and place. The following story is appropriate for that purpose:

I want to remind all of you that we are meeting again tomorrow morning at ten o'clock in the Lincoln Room on the third floor of this hotel. You may remember the little boy who came home from his first day at school and when his mother asked him the usual first day's question, "What did you learn in school today?", the boy answered, "Not much. I asked the teacher and she said yes, I have to come back tomorrow."

I thought we learned a lot today—but it's true, we're going to come back tomorrow anyhow; the Lincoln Room at ten a.m.

VOLUNTEERS NEEDED

(The purpose of your speech is to enlist volunteers.)

When enlisting volunteers for serving on committees, raising funds, obtaining new members, etc., you may want to use the following approach:

Let me explain why I am asking for volunteer help: There are about 210 million people in the United States whom I could call on for this, but I have to make numerous deductions from that figure. About 75 million of those people are over 70 years of age and may be too old to do this work. That leaves about 135 million people.

About 45 million of those are under 20 years of age. That leaves about 90 million people available to me.

But about 4 million of those are in the armed forces and that leaves only 86 million.

About 5 million of those are in hospitals and that leaves only 81 million.

And of those 81 million, I can state with confidence that 80,999,998 of them are just too lazy to do any work.

That leaves two—you and me. And I'm tired. Now you know whom that leaves. When can you start work?

Or you might like to use the following story:

When I talk to people about volunteering their services for the benefit of our organization, I think back on something I once read entitled "Essay on Fathers." It included both tributes and criticisms of fathers, all of them written by children.

The one which particularly interested me was this: "My father is never too tired to sit, sprawled out in his easy chair, and tell stories, while we children do the dishes."

I thought I would read that to you just to point up the fact that we don't need volunteers for story-telling; we need volunteers for getting members, collecting dues, writing letters, and for lots of other chores.

We are once again, as often happens, in dire need of volunteers. Whenever I bring up that subject, I always remember the big, burly truck driver who appeared one day at the dentist's office and asked him a question, "Doc, is it really true that you can pull a tooth and not hurt the patient at all?" And the dentist answered, "Of course it's true. You breathe a couple of whiffs of laughing gas and I pull the tooth and you don't feel a thing."

Said the trucker, "Is there an extra charge for that laughing gas?"

"Yes, there is a small charge—perhaps two or three dollars."

The trucker thought about that for a moment and then he said, "If that's the case, forget the laughing gas. Just pull the tooth even if it hurts a little bit more that way."

Said the dentist, "I certainly admire your attitude. You are a brave man. Get in the chair." Whereupon the trucker cried out, "Hold it! It's not me; it's my wife who's got the toothache!"

And to a great extent, that is the way it is with getting volunteers. They are quick to see the need for help and they think we ought to have the help, and most of the time they think the other fellow ought to furnish it.

However, I know, of course, that none of what I have said is true of this audience. And so I need only add that it would be appreciated if you would be patient and not push each other out of line or jostle each other trying to be the first to sign up for the volunteer work we need.

I have, of course, been addressing my remarks chiefly to the members of our organization. However, I note that many of you are not members—I prefer to say not *yet* members, because I hope you will be. But I want all of you who are guests of members to know that you are welcome as guests of our organization. I hope, of course, that you will feel moved to join us and to volunteer in work which I am sure you will find very rewarding.

Perhaps you have heard about the speaker who was regaling his audience with joke after joke, and who had everybody laughing uproariously—everybody, that is, except one man. All the others were holding their sides, while he was sitting motionless in his seat, straight faced and with his arms folded, not even smiling at any of the very funny stories. When the meeting broke up, the president of the organization sought out this man and said to him, "I noticed that you were the one person in this whole group who wasn't laughing. Was something wrong? Or did you just think the stories weren't funny?" And the man answered, "I thought the stories were just hilarious. But I felt that I didn't have any right to join in the laughter. I'm not a member."

I want to invite all our guests to join us in everything, including particularly the work we do. But if you laughed just now, perhaps you would feel more justified if you joined the organization and volunteered in its work!

Depending on the type of audience and the circumstances, a speaker sometimes feels that in appealing for volunteer help, a serious approach might be more fruitful than a humorous one. In that case, the following may be useful:

This is our organization and you and I have an obligation to it. This situation puts me in mind of the story about the Indian tribe some of the members of which had decided to embarrass the leader. They therefore insisted that the chief permit them to ask him a few questions in the presence of the whole tribe, and he consented.

For that purpose, one of the questioners had caught a small bird which he held concealed in the cup of his two hands. He then said to the chief, "You are thought to be a very wise man. Let's see how wise you are. Is the bird I hold concealed in my hands alive or dead?"

The questioner had planned that if the answer was "Alive," he would crush the bird and show that the chief was wrong. But if the answer was "Dead," he would open his hands and let the bird fly. Thus, either way, the chief would appear to lack wisdom.

However, the chief was indeed a wise man. He said only: "The answer is in your hands."

And so it is here, with your organization. If we do not fulfill our obligations, the organization may have a bleak future. If we work unselfishly so that it can accomplish its purposes, it will succeed—or, you might say, it will fly. The answer is in your hands.

[At the close of your explanation of the work to be done and the need for people to volunteer to do it:]

I know you are very busy. We all are. If you were not a person who is already interested in many kinds of things, if you were not already very busy, very concerned, very aware, I would not be appealing to you at all. There is an old saying to the effect that if you want a job to be done, go to the busiest man in town and he'll do it. I have also heard a modern version of that to the effect that if you want a job to be done, go to the busiest man in town—his secretary can handle it.

Anyhow, no matter how crowded your time already is, there's always room for one more project if you really feel the need of doing it. Our minds are never really filled.

You may remember the man who wanted to prove to his audience that there was always room for more. He started with an empty packing case. Then he opened package after package of billiard balls and dropped them into the packing case until it was full to the top. Then he said to the audience, "It is not really full." He then opened package after package of marbles and poured them in— and, of course, they dropped down through the crevices left by the billiard balls.

Then he said to the audience, "It is not really full." He then opened bags of buckshot and poured bag after bag of buckshot into that box. After which he said to the audience, "It is not really full."

He then poured a bucket of sand into the box and, of course, it worked down through all the spaces until you were sure the box was really full. But the man said, "It is not really full."

And finally he poured a bucket of water into the box and still the box did not overflow.

I think you will agree that the point made in this story is true of all of us. Our lives are extremely busy—but you and I know that there's room for one more deserving project.

WEATHER DISTRACTION

(Your audience is distracted by a sudden storm.)

The following story is applicable in any of several situations involving inclement weather—e.g., the noise of a storm disturbs the audience; a blizzard has prevented people from attending; thunder interrupts the speaking, etc.

I must interrupt myself to tell you that what is going on outside reminds me of the housewife who had invited a number of guests to her home for dinner and when they were all seated around the table, she stood in the doorway of the kitchen and said to her six-year-old son, "I think it would be nice if you said the blessing." The little boy thought a moment and then he said, "I don't know what to say." His mother answered, "Oh yes, you do. Just say what you've heard me say. It begins, 'Oh Lord, . . .' "

And so the little boy, bowing his head, said, "Oh Lord, why in the world did I invite these people here on a boiling hot day like this!"

I am sure some of you must be saying, "Oh Lord, why in the world did they invite me here on a stormy night like this!"

WEDDING ANNIVERSARIES

(You are to speak at a wedding anniversary.)

If you are to act as a master of ceremonies at a wedding party, even if others offer very serious, sometimes touching, comments about the bride, the groom, their parents, the future, you will furnish welcome relief if you can brighten the occasion with a bit of humor. For example:

> I think now I can disclose something that the bride did some time ago. She came down to the office [store, factory] one day and offered each man a cigar and each woman a candy bar, with blue ribbons attached. Now, her co-workers all knew that she was single, and everybody asked what the occasion was. She answered, "It's a boy. Six feet tall and 185 pounds!"

If you are either the MC or just "a member of the wedding," you may feel called upon to offer a toast to the bride and groom. Most toasts are ordinary and uninteresting—too much like everybody else's. A toast, to be successful, should have a little sparkle. You might use one of these:

> I read some place, long ago, that a married couple is like a pair of scissors. They sometimes oppose each other, might even make cutting remarks. But if anyone tries to come between them, heaven help him! And I feel that this is particularly appropriate today, because the bride and groom are both so sharp!

Either added to the foregoing, or alone, the following can be offered:

Helen and George, I wish you three "h"s. (You know I would not give you H- - -, but I will give you three "h"s.) They stand for Health, Happiness and Hilarity. And don't forget that third one, because it helps you get the other two.

Or, in the alternative:

Helen and George, I wish you three "l"s. (You know I would not give you - - -l, but I will give you three "l"s.) They stand for Love, Longevity and Laughter. And don't forget that third one, because it helps you get the other two.

At a wedding celebration, if you are the MC, and if you are very well acquainted with most of the people present and you know that "spoofing" the bride and groom will be enjoyed by your audience (and by the bride and groom!), you will find all— or any part—of the following will fit the occasion:

This is a very happy celebration and we all know that the bride and groom are well suited to each other. However, we all know, too, that husbands and wives do occasionally have misunderstandings or fail to see eye to eye. (And now, I happen to know that this is the universal situation in all husband and wife situations—except, of course, my own. In fact, just by making that exception, I have averted such a situation!) Knowing all this, I feel that I ought to give the bride and groom some tips for the future:

They must remember that there is always a solution for every problem. For instance, take the case of the man whose wife was forever moving the furniture around the living room, and always with the help of her husband's muscle. He didn't want to rebel and simply refuse to help her, but he did want to find some other solution—and he found it.

She went on a visit to a relative in another city for a few days, and while she was gone, he redecorated the apartment, repapering every room. When she returned, she loved it—said it was beautiful, exclaimed over it. But she did think that the sofa would be better over there and the big upholstered chair over here. As they pulled the heavy sofa away from the wall, she gasped and put it back. That part of the wall behind the sofa, and all other portions of the walls behind the big pieces of furniture, had been left blank. That was the end of her penchant for furniture moving. You see, problems can be solved.

Of course, she retaliated, but in a quite different way. A few days later she showed him the ad she had put in the newspaper. It read, "For sale, full set of *Encyclopedia Britannica*. Hardly used; good as new. My husband knows all about everything."

I must also warn the groom—and in fact all husbands—about the efficiency expert who applied his time-saving methods at home. He later related to a young man in his office what he had done. He had showed his wife several ways of saving many steps and much energy. For example, he showed her that carrying the silver and plates and napkins together, from the cupboard to the table, instead of making several trips, saved a lot of steps. In telling about it, this efficiency expert finally ended by saying: "I must advise you, however, not to apply your time studies at home. What my wife used to do in 17 minutes, I now do in six."

WOMAN

(The speaker is a woman.)

When the speaker is a woman, the chairman introducing her must be careful to do so with all the deference he would use in introducing a man. Nevertheless, an anecdote in which the chief character is a woman is not out of place if in good taste. And the audience often welcomes it, provided always that the speaker is never the butt of the story. Depending upon the audience and the speaker, you might wish to use one of the following:

> In introducing our speaker, Miss Blank, let me tell you a little story which you will quickly realize has no application whatever. A neighbor of mine told me recently that during a heavy thunderstorm his little boy said to him, "Daddy, aren't you afraid of the thunder and the lightning?" Naturally my friend's answer was, "Why, of course not!" Whereupon the little boy said, "Oh Daddy, aren't you afraid of anything in the world except only Mama?"
>
> As you listen to Miss Blank you will agree with me that the story is not pertinent at all—although I hope it is not impertinent!—because when you listen to the calm, gentle, intelligent Miss Blank you may be filled with admiration but certainly not with fear.

With the same introductory words about its nonrelevance you may prefer to use one of the following:

At a large party of married folks not long ago the hostess, just for fun, announced that all the husbands who felt that they were dominated by their wives should gather at one side of the room and those who felt they dominated their wives should gather on the other side. After a few minutes it was obvious that all the men but one had lined up on the side which indicated that in their opinion their wives dominated them. But on the other side of the room was one lone little man. The hostess, thinking he might have misunderstood, went to him and said, "Do you feel that you dominate your wife?" And he answered, "Sure I do, but my wife wouldn't let me go to that other side of the room."

Miss Blank works with persuasion, not with domination. She doesn't demand agreement; she wins it by the cogency of her argument.

Not too long ago I heard a woman say, "My husband and I have been married for fifteen years, and we have never quarreled. That's because when we have a difference of opinion and I'm right and my husband is wrong, he frankly admits it and gives in." And someone asked, "But what happens when your husband is right?" She thought about that for a moment and then she said, "I really don't know the answer to that—it has never happened in all these fifteen years."

Or do you prefer the following version:

Not too long ago I heard a woman say, "My husband and I have been married for fifteen years and we have always gotten along beautifully. That's because whenever a matter of real importance comes up I let him decide it, and

I decide all the unimportant matters." And someone asked, "Well, does he decide the important matters correctly?" And she answered, "That's hard to say because in all these fifteen years not a single matter of importance has come up."

I know this is not Mrs. Blank's idea of division of labor, because she is talking to us today on something that we all recognize is a very important matter. And she is about to handle it herself.

Some women are commanding and domineering—they are altogether different from our speaker—and it's about one of those I want to tell you. A husband and his domineering wife were partners in a bridge game and the husband made a grand slam, doubled and redoubled. Triumphantly he turned to his wife and said, "And you thought I couldn't make it, didn't you?" "Well, dear," she answered, "You couldn't have if you had played it right."

Not only is Mrs. Blank totally unlike the lady I have just told you about, but she plays her cards right—as you will readily agree when you hear her speak on the subject of _____.

A friend of mine was doing a bit of carpentry. His little girl was watching him, asking questions, making observations, and being a general nuisance. Finally her father said, "Now, Daddy is measuring, so be quiet." And the little girl answered, "I don't have to be quiet—I'm a woman."

Miss Blank, you don't have to be quiet either. But that's not because you're a woman. It's because we are happy to have you with us today and eager to hear what you have to tell us.

◆—◆—◆—◆—◆

Our speaker this evening is Mrs. Blank. She is very well known and highly respected in her field. The extent of her reputation reminds me of an occurrence involving Franklin Roosevelt. You may recall that Roosevelt, while he was President, made a trip to Africa and was driven through the streets of an African village. The natives lined the roads and many of them shouted something which he could not understand, but which sounded like, "Calado, rumayo, tola!" Later, he asked one of the diplomats what that meant, and the answer was, "That's her husband! That's her husband!"

I do want to reassure Mr. Blank that I don't think Mrs. Blank's reputation has quite reached the point where Mr. Blank would be identified in the same way. But it is certainly true that Mrs. Blank is widely recognized and admired by her colleagues.

Some time ago, the Duke of Edinburgh made a trip to the United States and Canada without his wife, the Queen of England.

At a private party in New York given in his honor, the guests were introduced to the duke. One couple was introduced as "Mr. and Dr. Young." The duke looked puzzled, and Mr. Young explained, "My wife is a doctor; I am not. She's recognized as much more important than I am." And the duke answered, "What a coincidence! Same situation as in our family!"

Our next speaker is a woman. I don't think we ought to make the mistake of assuming that she is a rabid Women's Libber. Nevertheless, she probably does have fairly definite views about the place of women in modern society—as most of us do. However, she is no doubt aware that although many men are ready to accord women an equal place in the world, many males are still hard to convince. I warned her that there may be some of those in this audience, and I am ready to give her an example:

I overheard a neighbor of mine who raised his voice in revolt. He shouted, "I want a little consideration around here. I want kindness and I want respect! And I want plenty of hot water! I tell you right now I won't wash dishes in cold water for any woman."

So I look to the speaker to remember that there are Male Libbers like that everywhere. And this is still true despite the fact that all of us males know that the philosopher was right who said to an audience of men, "If you are ever in doubt as to who is standing in your home as the head of the household, just pick up your apron and look at your own two feet."

A young husband, soon to be a father, was pacing the floor waiting for word from the nurse. Finally she appeared and said, "I am happy to tell you that your wife has just given birth to a possible future president of the United States." And then she promptly added, "That is, provided we get smart enough to elect a woman."

In these days of equality for women, I suppose I should introduce our next speaker without referring in any way to his or her sex. I am not going to be that modern, because if I were, I wouldn't be able to tell you about the little boy in sixth grade who wrote a theme in his physiology class, which included this sentence: "Anatomy is something everybody's got—but it sure looks better on a girl."

I must at once assure you and our speaker that this little boy's observation was not even in our minds when we extended our invitation to her. She is here because she is a recognized expert in her field and she would have been selected as our speaker even if she didn't prove that little boy's very astute comment.

As you know, our speaker tonight is a woman. With the Women's Lib Movement advancing so successfully, a woman is assured of special attention. Even before Women's Lib attracted so much support, women never suffered from lack of attention, it seems to me, and this was true at every stage of life.

Just think for a moment: When a man is born, people ask at once, "How's the mother?" When he gets married, people say, "Doesn't the bride look beautiful!", and when he dies, all that people say is, "How much did he leave her?"

And so I have no doubt that our speaker tonight will have your full attention; but I want particularly to add that you will find she deserves it.

I know you have often heard the warning, "Never underestimate the power of a woman."

In that connection I must tell you of the man who telephoned his Lodge and asked if there was to be a meeting of the Lodge that evening. The answer was: "No. It had to be postponed. The grand, exalted, invincible Potentate of the Lodge could not make the meeting. His wife wouldn't let him out tonight."

I hasten to assure you that the lady who is our speaker this evening could never be guilty of such overt, dictatorial conduct as I have just described. For example, she could never be guilty of the kind of angry statement made by a wife who screamed at her husband:

"For weeks I have been telling you not to buy me anything for my birthday—and still you forgot to buy me something."

She is a much more subtle person, you may be sure. However, the original warning not to underestimate her still stands.

I know that a chairman introducing a speaker should be reminded of only one story at most. But I am breaking that rule on this occasion because our speaker tonight reminds me of two stories. However, fortunately for you, they are both very short.

First, I am reminded of a cartoon I saw recently which showed two little boys watching a little girl as she passed by, and one of them was saying to the other, "Well, if I ever stop hating girls, she's the one I am going to stop hating first."

The truth is that I stopped hating girls a long time ago but if I had met the speaker way back when, I might have stopped hating girls earlier.

The other story of which I am reminded is about the boy who sent a little card along with the first orchid he had ever bought. It said, "With all my heart and nearly all my allowance."

And that story also tells the way I feel about the lady I am now presenting. I would give my whole allowance any time just to hear her speak.

In introducing the lady who is to speak to us this evening, I am reminded of the man who was applying for a job and answering the questions put to him by his prospective employer. When he was asked whether he was married, his answer was in the nature of a lengthy speech about what a wonderful woman his wife was. He described her as quiet, unassuming, beautiful, intelligent, calm and cool, helpful, unselfish—until finally the interviewer interrupted him and said: "Too bad you didn't bring her along so I could meet her."

The reply was, "No, no. It is much better that I didn't. If I had, you would have been dissatisfied for the rest of your life." At the risk of all the men in this audience being dissatisfied for the rest of their lives, I introduce Miss Blank.

Because the next speaker is a woman, I am reminded of a little boy who asked his father whether men were smarter than women or vice versa. The father's answer was, "Son, you know that men are much smarter than women."

This led to another question: "Well, then, are you smarter than Mom?" To this the father replied: "Of course I am! "

The boy thought about that for a moment and then he said, "Is it all right if I tell that to Mom?" And the father answered, "I wouldn't do that because I don't think Mom is smart enough to know that I am smarter."

Tonight we have the reverse situation. I pride myself on being smart enough to know that your speaker is much smarter than I am.

In introducing the lady who is our speaker this evening, I must make a confession: I sometimes wonder whether, in some ways, Women's Lib has perhaps been too successful. I wonder whether it has to an extent made men—some men—feel less venturous, less capable, even less than equal. You may remember the father who was asked by his small son, "Why is there a law that a man cannot have more than one wife?" And the father's answer was: "When you get older, you will realize that the law protects those who are incapable of protecting themselves."

Along the same line, I remember the young man who was finally able to land an acting part in a play. He was very elated and he promptly told his father, "I got the job. I am going to play the part of a man who has been married for thirty years."

"Oh," said the father. "That's not bad for a beginner. And if you are good, maybe next time they will give you a speaking part."

Tonight, the speaking part is to be played by a woman—our guest speaker of the evening.

In introducing our speaker this evening, I want first to tell you about the big strapping fellow from Texas who applied for a job at the employment office of a large corporation in New York. He handed the interviewer the application form which he had filled out and which included the fact that he had seven children. The interviewer looked up and said, "That's funny. I am one of seven myself. I have three brothers and three sisters."

"Oh," said the applicant. "If you count girls, I have eleven children."

I want to assure our speaker that here we do count girls. And sometimes, as in her case, we rate them very high.

The following lead-in is appropriate for introducing any woman speaker irrespective of background, education, occupation, etc.

I am informed that the laws of India provide that it is permissible and entirely legal to tell a lie in two kinds of situation: one, to save a life; two, to compliment a woman.

Fortunately, I don't need either exemption this evening when it comes to complimenting the lady who is our speaker this evening. I can compliment her and yet tell only the truth.

Some time ago, a new prime minister of Australia was elected. He was promptly interviewed about various matters, including particularly whom he intended to name as his cabinet officers. One of the reporters put it this way: "Sir, in making your decisions, will you be consulting the powerful influences who were responsible for your becoming prime minister?"

His immediate answer was, "Young man, I will thank you for keeping my wife out of this."

Many a successful man would, if he spoke the truth, answer similarly.

And that brings me logically to the introduction of one of those powerful influences.

Before going into the actual introduction of a woman speaker—her education, background, reputation, etc.—you may wish to say a word about the progress women have made in recent years in gaining increased recognition. For example:

I suppose very few women consider that Woman's Lib has gone too far. But an occasional male may find some such evil thought crossing his mind.

I remember the man who confided to a friend that he was disappointed that his wife gave birth to a daughter.

"Gosh," he said, "I was hoping for a boy to help me with the housework."

WRONG TOPIC

(There has been a misunderstanding about the subject of your speech.)

Sometimes, especially when arrangements are made over the telephone without confirmation in writing, there is a misunderstanding as to the subject of your speech, and the audience has been led to expect a talk on a different subject. You may wish to include the following in your explanation:

Mistakes will happen—and one has happened in connection with my talk this evening. I know you came in response to an announcement to the effect that I would be speaking to you about _____. I must in some way have misled your chairman when we were discussing this event. I understood that I was to talk to you on the subject of _____.

I hope you will forgive this misunderstanding. It can happen to any of us. You may remember that the famous actor, Monte Woolley, was an irascible old fellow who usually made himself very clear. But on one occasion he was wholly misunderstood. When he checked out of the hotel where he had spent several days, he asked for the manager. When confronted by him, Mr. Woolley handed him a beautiful bouquet of flowers, saying, "These are for your switchboard operators." The manager was very pleased. He said, "Mr. Woolley, the operators will be delighted to have these." Woolley's answer was, "They'll be delighted to have these! I thought they were dead!"

At least our misunderstanding carries no innuendos whatever.

As you know, mistakes do happen. The program says one thing but I am going to be saying something else. I don't know whose error it was—perhaps mine—but in any case, it's of no great consequence. I can cite worse errors; for instance, I recall that when the First National Bank in my home town moved across the street, the newspaper said, "The transfer of business of the First National Bank was effected this week without the slightest interruption of confusion."

And even worse than that was one of the reports in the newspaper when President Eisenhower had a heart attack. The paper said, "Dr. Paul Dudley White, the President's heart specialist, today outlined a six-pint program to be followed by the President."

In our case, the title of my talk should have been "_____."

As we all know, mistakes will happen. The chairman of your program committee and I apparently misunderstood each other when we were arranging for my presence here this evening. The situation reminds me of the husband who brought home to his wife a little card he had obtained from one of those weighing machines that give your weight and also your fortune. She read the card aloud. It said, "You are a leader of men. You are intelligent, industrious and dynamic, and you have great strength of character." And then she said, "Oh my! They've got your weight wrong too!"

In this case, it isn't that bad. All the flattering adjectives your chairman used in introducing me may be highly inaccurate but I think he has my weight about right. The only difficulty is that your chairman is about to hear a speech on a different topic than he expected. [Then explain the misunderstanding.]

APPENDIX

APPENDIX: HANDY HUMOR FOR ANY OCCASION

It is unquestionably true that a story that is appropriate to the current situation or event carries far more punch than just "a funny story." Nevertheless, in an informal gathering it sometimes happens that one is asked whether he has heard any good stories lately. This is particularly likely to occur when one has become recognized as an effective toastmaster with something of a reputation for the aptness of his stories.

On these occasions it is hardly possible to tell a story that has any connection with the current situation, but there are anecdotes that are funny enough in themselves to warrant telling. One of the following will serve the purpose very well:

One of the bosses in a middlewestern factory was about to be married. A young man in the office was designated to take up a collection and get him a gift. He made the rounds of the entire factory over a period of about two weeks and asked forty cents from each of one thousand employees—a total of four hundred dollars.

Without saying anything to any of the employees he bought one thousand packs of cigarets with that four hundred dollar fund—the kind of cigarets that give gift coupons. He then turned in the thousand coupons for a beautiful silver coffee service. That was the wedding gift. But to each of the employees he returned a package of cigarets.

The bridegroom somehow heard of the ingenious plan that produced the beautiful silver wedding gift. He called in the young man and complimented him on his cleverness, and he said to him, "You really ought to have some reward for thinking up such a scheme. My wife and I got a beautiful silver coffee service and all the employees got a package of cigarets for their forty-cent contribution. You ought to get something for that." Said the young man, "Well, to tell the truth, I did get something for myself. You see, I bought the cigarets at a store where they give trading stamps. For that four hundred dollars I got four thousand trading stamps, and I cashed those in for a complete fishing outfit."

Mr. Baker and Mr. Henderson had completed a business transaction in Mr. Baker's office. In the course of it, Mr. Baker had sent his office boy out on an errand which the office boy had misunderstood and therefore executed badly. Mr. Henderson took the matter lightly, however, and merely said," I thought I had the dumbest office boy but perhaps your boy is a candidate for that title." Said Mr. Baker, "You have no idea how dumb this boy is. I'll call him in and you just listen to the errand I'll be sending him on."

When the boy came in, Mr. Baker handed the boy a nickel and said to him, "Take this and go to the nearest Cadillac agency and buy me a Cadillac right away." "Yes, sir," said the boy politely and went on his way.

Said Mr. Henderson, "I agree that your boy is pretty bad, but if I may use your telephone, I'd like to have you hear the errand I'll send my boy on." Mr. Henderson then phoned his own office, asked for his office boy, and said to him, "I'm calling you from outside the office. You know where my club is. Please go to the club and see if I'm there "

A few minutes later the two office boys, who happened to be acquainted, met by accident on the street. One of them said to the other, "I've got the dumbest boss you ever heard of." The other one said, "Don't you believe it. *I* have the dumbest boss in the world and I'll prove it to you: He just called me in his office and gave me a nickel and told me to go buy him a Cadillac. Not a word about whether I am to get a two-door or a four-door; I don't know what color he wants. That's what you call dumb." But the first boy answered, "You ain't heard nuthin' yet. My boss is out of the office. He just phoned me and asked me to go down to his club and see if he's there. But look— he phoned me, didn't he? Then why didn't he phone the club and save me this trip?"

A star guard on a college football team knew that he was going to be flunked out and would be ineligible for the big game the following Saturday. So he went to his coach and asked him if by any chance he could intercede for him so that he might play.

The coach said, "I ain't very good at this, but I'll try. The dean is a former football player so there's a chance."

A few days later, the coach explained the arrangements he had made. He said, "The dean is going to give you a one-question final examination. If you pass it, you'll be eligible. If you don't, you're through."

The following day, the star player and his coach came to the dean's office for the one-question test. Said the dean, "How much are 7 and 7?" The young man thought about that for a time and then he said, "13."

The dean, shaking his head sadly, turned to the coach and said, "How can I pass this man on that answer?"

"Dean!" shouted the coach. "You're not going to flunk this fellow just because he missed it by two!"

Like so many others of us, Jack Henderson not only was a good golfer; he lived and breathed golf. With the passage of time he began to wonder whether there would be a good golf course in heaven. If there were not, he decided that he might favor the other possible destination.

One day he determined to make inquiries about it and he went to the local priest and asked him for an introduction to the archbishop in that diocese.

An appointment was made for him and with due deference he presented himself at the designated time. He explained to the archbishop: "I love golf. I play it every minute of every day that I can afford to be at the links. I expect to go to heaven some day and I would hope to find there a beautiful golf course. I understand that you have a working relationship with some of the saints and if you could get an opportunity to find out from Saint Peter whether heaven has a golf course, perhaps his answer would set my mind at rest."

The archbishop answered, "I shall try, my son. Come back in two weeks and I may have your answer."

Two weeks later, Jack Henderson was again in the archbishop's presence. He asked at once, "You have good news for me, Father?" The archbishop's answer was: "I have good news and bad news. The good news is that there is indeed a golf course in heaven. It is beautiful— magnificent. The grass never needs cutting; it remains at the perfect height always, on the greens and in the fairways. That's the good news."

Said Henderson, "Don't tell me, Father, that the bad news is that for some reason I can't play on it!"

"Not at all," said the archbishop. "The bad news is that Saint Peter has you down for teeing off day after tomorrow."

An elderly gentleman came into a supermarket and asked the clerk in the vegetable section whether he could buy half a head of lettuce. The young man answered that he would have to ask the manager and he promptly walked to the rear of the store where the manager was working. Without his knowing it, he was being followed by his customer. Unaware of the old gentleman's presence, he said to the manager, "There's a screwball in the vegetable section who wants to buy half a head of lettuce." Then suddenly seeing his customer standing nearby, he quickly said, "And this gentleman is ready to take the other half, so I suppose it's all right, isn't it?"

The manager said, "Certainly." And the clerk then went back to his section and completed the sale.

A few minutes later, the manager appeared and said to the clerk, "You got out of that very neatly. I understood what was happening—and you thought quickly enough to get yourself out of trouble. Nice work!"

Said the young man, "Well, that old guy must have been a Canadian. Canadians are funny people—especially people from Quebec."

"What's the matter with people from Quebec?" asked the manager. Said the clerk, "Everybody from Quebec is either a hockey player or a prostitute—everybody."

"Wait a minute," said the manager with some hostility. "My wife came from Quebec!" Whereupon the young clerk answered, "She did? That's interesting! What hockey team did she play on?"

A newspaper reporter decided to visit the state mental hospital to determine whether patients were being properly treated. When he entered the hospital, the first person he saw was an elderly man who was sweeping the floor. "Are you a patient here?" the reporter asked. "No," said the man. "I work here. I have been working here for about twenty years."

"During that long time, have you taken on some of the ideas that these patients have?" asked the reporter. "No," was the answer. "I know that some of the long-time employees have done that, but I never have."

The reporter then noticed that hanging high above them from the ceiling was a patient who was in no pain whatever and seemed to be satisfied where he was. And at that moment a doctor came walking down the hall. The reporter stopped him at once and asked him about the man who was hanging from the ceiling. "Oh, he's all right," said the doctor. "He thinks he's an electric light bulb, and he's much happier up there. However, I'm going to have my daily session with him now, and so I'm going to take him down and we'll have a talk in my office."

The doctor then reached up and twisted the man around several times and brought him down. Together they walked down the hall toward the doctor's office with the reporter following after them. The reporter then noticed that the janitor was coming along, too. Turning to him, the reporter asked, "Are you going to have a session with the doctor, too?"

"Of course not," said the janitor. "It's just that I can't work back there in the dark."

An American traveler in Italy decided to have a suit made while he was there. Seeing some material that he liked very much and that he was assured was amply sufficient for a suit, he bought it and then went at once to a tailor shop near his hotel.

The tailor examined the material and then said, "It's very nice, but there isn't enough for a suit."

The gentleman, deciding that he had been taken and planning to return the material to the shop where he had bought it, happened to see another tailor shop on his way. He decided to stop at that shop, if only to verify the fact that there was not enough material for a suit.

This second tailor examined the cloth, spoke admiringly of it and proceeded to take the man's measurements.

"Is there enough material?" asked the customer. "Plenty," said the tailor. "Plenty for coat, trousers and vest. Come back two weeks from today and I'll have your suit."

Two weeks later, the visitor came to the tailor shop and, upon opening the door, he was astonished to see a little boy, playing on the floor of the shop, dressed in a little suit obviously made out of the material left there two weeks before.

As soon as the tailor saw him, he brought out the beautiful three-piece suit he had promised. It fit perfectly.

Said the customer: "There's something I don't understand. Before I came in here, I stopped at Garibaldi's, but he told me that there wasn't enough material. You have not only made me a suit which fits perfectly, but you had enough material to make your little boy a suit, I notice. How do you explain that?"

"Easily," answered the tailor. "Garibaldi couldn't take the job. He has twin boys."

◆◆◆◆

Walking down the street, Jones ran into Smith and stopped to greet him. "What in the world happened to you, Smith?" he asked. "Both your cheeks are fiery red as if they had been burned!"

Said Smith, "Here's what happened: A few nights ago, I came home dead drunk. In that condition, I got the silly idea of pressing a couple of suits, so I got out the ironing board and plugged in the electric iron. Without noticing it, I left the iron, while it was heating up, right next to the telephone. And a little later the phone rang. You can guess what I did, considering my condition. I picked up the iron instead of the telephone, put it to my ear, and in the process burned my cheek something awful." Jones said a few sympathetic words and then he added, "That must have been pretty bad—but both your cheeks look burned. What happened to the other cheek?"

"Well," answered Smith, "I had to call the doctor, didn't I?"

A surgeon, an engineer and a congressman were arguing about which of their respective professions was first established on Earth.

The surgeon proudly called the attention of the others to the fact that Eve was created out of Adam's rib. Thus, surgery was the first profession.

But the engineer said, "Before Adam, the Earth was created out of chaos in six days. That was an engineering problem. Engineering was the earliest profession."

Said the congressman, "Wait, gentlemen, stop and think. Who created that chaos if it wasn't the congressmen!"

Three animals, a horse, a cow and a jackass, were asking about their respective contributions to the world war.

Said the horse: "I made the greatest contribution to the war. I pulled the artillery and I also carried the generals—mostly in parades, of course."

Said the cow: "What you did was of very little consequence. But I furnished milk to the troops and to the war workers and to all their families at home."

Said the jackass: "Neither of you contributed anywhere near as much as I did. If it hadn't have been for jackasses, we would not have had any war at all."

A man entered a taxi at the airport and the driver promptly took off at a wild pace, turning corners on two wheels, crossing intersections on the yellow light and barely missing safety islands. Noting in the rear-view mirror that his passenger seemed to be disturbed, the driver reassured him. "Don't worry, sir," he said. "Nothing will happen. I was in the Army and I spent a whole year in the hospital, and I am not anxious to go back to one."

"A year in the hospital!" said his fare. "You must have been very seriously wounded."

"No," said the driver. "Not a scratch. I was a mental case."

At a meeting which took place on a certain April Fool's Day, the subject appropriately assigned to the speaker was "Fools."

In introducing the speaker, the chairman said, "We are now to hear a talk on 'Fools' by one . . ." and he was interrupted by a gale of laughter. When it had subsided, he added, " . . . of the wisest men I have ever met."

The speaker, not to be outdone, began by saying, "Ladies and gentlemen, I am not as big a fool as your chairman . . ." and again there were gales of laughter, which he interrupted by finishing with " . . . would have you believe I am."

A wholesale jeweler and one of his retail customers carried on a series of bargaining sessions over a very beautiful emerald necklace. The former wanted to sell and the latter wanted to buy—but they could not agree on price.

Finally, to resolve the difficulty, the wholesaler sent the necklace, by insured mail, beautifully packed in a jewel case with a letter stating that the price was $20,000, that there was no room for further bargaining and that if the retailer did not wish to pay that price he was simply to mail the necklace back to the wholesaler and the matter could be dropped.

In about a week, a package arrived on the wholesaler's desk with a letter. The letter contained a check for $15,000 and stated: "I realize you said not to try to bargain, but the necklace is worth only $15,000. If you accept my check in full payment, all you need to do is just re-address the package without opening it. Of course, if you still insist on the $20,000 price, simply open the package and return our $15,000 check."

The wholesaler, now very angry, and insistent upon getting the full price, tore open the package ready to restore the necklace to his stock. The package contained only a check for $5,000 with a little note which said, "Don't get excited. Here's the rest of your money."

A man was going through the pockets of his old suits before discarding them and he came upon a claim-check that had been given to him by a shoemaker when he had left his shoes to be repaired almost ten years earlier.

On making that discovery the man said to himself, "I know that shop. I remember leaving my shoes there years ago to be repaired. I don't believe I ever picked them up, or I would not have this check in my pocket. Perhaps it will turn out to be a foolish errand, but I am going back to that shop and see if they still have my shoes."

The following day he presented himself at the shoe repair shop, handed the claim-check to the shoemaker and said very apologetically, "I know this check is very old, but I have never picked up those shoes. Would you please look to see if you still have them."

The shoemaker went back to his shelves of repaired shoes, saying, half aloud, "A ten-year old check! People bring their shoes in, forget all about them, and then come in ten years later and expect to get them! How irresponsible can they get!"

After a few minutes of digging through the many pairs of shoes on the shelves, the shoemaker turned to his customer and said, "I think I have them. Tan shoes? Wing tips? Soles and heels to be done?"

"Yes," said the man, "those are my shoes!"

"OK," said the shoemaker. "Come in next Tuesday afternoon and I will have them for you."

A young man and a young girl decided to get married, because they believed they owed that to their one-year-old child. They went to a lawyer who told them that under the laws of their state this could be quietly handled by signing a sworn petition—without their going to court and with no ceremony.

Accordingly, the petition was filed. But when the lawyer presented it in court the judge insisted, despite the lawyer's objections, on the lawyer's producing the girl in court so that the judge could make sure she understood what was being done.

Accordingly, the lawyer brought her into court. After some preliminary remarks by the judge he said to the young woman, "You understand, do you not, that in spite of this proceeding your little son will still be a technical bastard. And do you know what that is?"

"Oh yes," she said. "That's what the lawyer said you are."

A teacher who was anxious to have her class thinking more broadly and with some historical perspective, tried a new assignment. She asked each of them to list the names of the nine greatest living persons.

After a considerable time, all of her pupils had handed in their lists except one little boy. She found Tommy with pen in hand, frowning, apparently still trying to complete his list. "Having trouble, Tommy?" the teacher asked.

Said Tommy: "Well, I'm satisfied with the first eight names, but I am having a hard time picking a shortstop."

A Hollander and an American were trading information about the burden of taxes in their respective countries.

Said the Dutchman: "Both your flag and ours are red, white, and blue. Here, in Holland, we say that our taxes remind us of our flag because we get red in the face when we think about taxes, we get white with rage when the tax bill comes, and we have to pay till we get blue in the face."

The American answered: "It's just the same in the United States, but under our flag we see stars, too!"

An office boy approached his boss. "Could I ask you a question, sir?"

The boss assured him he could. "Well," said the boy, "it's really none of my business, but I would like to ask who those two ladies were who came to the office yesterday."

"Certainly," was the answer. "They were Marilyn Monroe and my wife."

The boy hesitated for a moment and then he asked, "Which one was Marilyn Monroe?"

The boss promptly pulled a five-dollar bill from his pocket and handed it to the boy. "What's this for?" asked the boy.

Said the boss: "When you are president of the company—and that will probably happen soon—I want you to remember I was good to you."